John Evans 10.8

CW01651142

GCSE

Science

Higher

Series Editor
Alan Brewerton

Authors
John Dobson
Paul Levy
Nick Parmar

Revision Notes

Letts
EDUCATIONAL

First published 1997

Letts Educational, Aldine House, Aldine Place, London W12 8AW
0181 740 2266

Editorial, design and production by Hart McLeod, Cambridge

British Library Cataloguing-in-Publication Data
A CIP record for this book is available from the British Library

ISBN 1 85758 644 1

Printed and bound in Great Britain by The Burlington Press Ltd

Letts Educational is the trading name of BPP (Letts Educational) Ltd

Acknowledgements
The author and publishers are grateful to the staff at Cottenham Village College, Cambridge for their technical assistance.

Contents

Introduction

Using this book

Your Revision Notes will help you remember your work in the easiest way possible – by reducing the information to a series of brief facts and explanations. These will refresh your memory and help in understanding the subject and organising your revision programme.

This book also contains key tips from examiners and spaces for you to write in your own additional comments. Each section is supplemented by a short test to ensure you have covered the topic sufficiently.

Keep this book with you throughout your revision – it is your key to success. Revising your work and planning for examinations are two vital steps on the path to GCSE success. This is a summary of the information you need.

Start your preparation now, by planning your work

In most subjects you will have:

- coursework
- homework
- revision
- practice examination questions
- an examination.

The examination may cause you most anxiety. With proper preparation, however, examinations need not be feared.

Make a list of what you have to do and write down coursework deadlines. Find out dates of examinations and arrange a revision timetable. Use your homework timetable to make a plan.

Divide your time between homework, coursework and learning. Be prepared to work at weekends but also include time to relax, keep fit and enjoy yourself.

Revise several subjects each day – in 30 minute sessions

Short bursts of revision in a variety of subjects are better than trying to revise one subject for a long time.

Get into the habit of revising at set times

Choose whichever is best for you – early morning, in the evening or during the early hours. People cannot concentrate well for more than 30 minutes. Break for about 10 minutes between each half-hour session. Thirty minutes of maximum concentration is better than an hour in which your mind wanders.

Understand your work

Make sure you understand important concepts. Explaining to a relative or friend is a good test. Discuss topics with a friend. If you don't understand ask your teacher. Make sure you understand important words e.g. work – the movement of a force through a distance.

Learn your work

Writing down or reading notes out loud often helps learning. Try to remember by telling another person about it. Repeat the exercise until you can remember what you have learned.

Use practice questions

There is a limit to the questions examiners can ask. The more you practise the less likely you are to be caught out. Remember, questions fall into three categories:

- knowledge – easily answered if you have learned your work
- understanding – easily answered if you have understood your work
- problem solving – testing your skill at using knowledge to interpret information.

If you answer structured questions, where one part leads on to the next or several short answers are needed, answer in sequence. If you tackle longer response questions, plan what you wish to say and say it without waffling.

Most of all

Good luck with your revision and your examinations.

Life processes & living things

Life processes & cell activity

Characteristics of living things

Biology – **science of living things**.

- **Zoology** – study of **animals.**
- **Botany** – study of **plants.**
- **Microbiology** – study of **bacteria**, **viruses**, and **fungi**.

To be considered as living, *all* of the following **seven characteristics must be present**. Some non-living things have some of these characteristics but never all seven, e.g. a car can move, respire and feed (use oxygen to burn fuel) but it is *not* alive!

Remember these by the phrase MRS FERG: movement respiration sensitivity feeding excretion reproduction growth

- **Movement** – living things can move – animals their whole bodies – plants parts of their bodies, e.g. leaves turn towards the Sun, flowers can open and close.
- **Respiration** – **release of energy from food** – essential to all life – provides energy to carry out living functions – most organisms use oxygen to respire.
- **Sensitivity** – living things detect and respond to changes in the environment – animals respond quickly by moving – plants usually respond slowly by growing.
- **Feeding** – all living things need food – provides **energy** through respiration and other essential substances, e.g. proteins, minerals etc.
- **Excretion** – removal from body of waste products, e.g. urea, carbon dioxide, water, from chemical reactions inside cells. *Note* It is *not* removal of waste from digestion – this is called **egestion** or **elimination**.
- **Reproduction** – all living things produce young – plants and animals reproduce so that species continues after they die.
- **Growth** – all living things increase in size – animals grow until adult – some plants never stop growing.

Cells

All living things are made up of cells

Each living thing *may be* made up of millions of cells or just one cell, e.g. simple animal called Amoeba.

Animal cells

It is very important to learn the names of the parts of plant and animal cells.

All animal cells have three basic parts:

- **cell membrane** – outside wall of cell – allows certain chemicals to move in and out of cell.
- **cytoplasm** – contains many tiny structures which keep cell alive.
- **nucleus** – control centre of cell – contains chemical information needed to make living thing. *Note* Human red blood cells do *not* have nuclei – more space to carry oxygen.

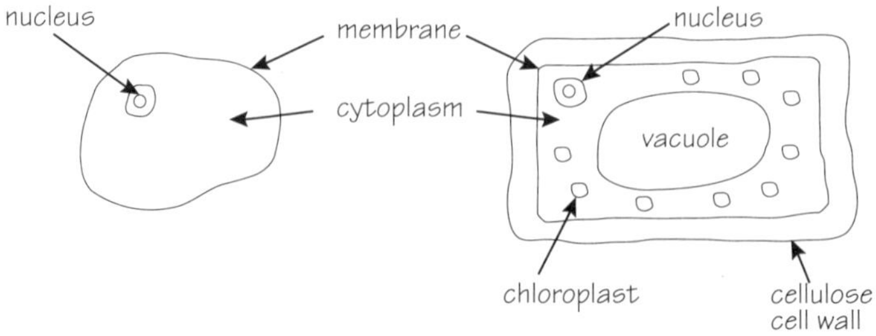

Plant cells

Plant cells contain all **features of animal cells**, but can have **some extra ones**:

Test yourself! Can you draw and label the cells without looking? *This is important!*

- **Cellulose Cell Wall –** gives plant cell strength – makes it tough and rigid.
- **Vacuole** – a space filled with water – when full of water the plant cell is strong and rigid – said to be **turgid**.
- **Chloroplasts** – contains green **chlorophyll** – absorbs light which plant uses to make food to grow.

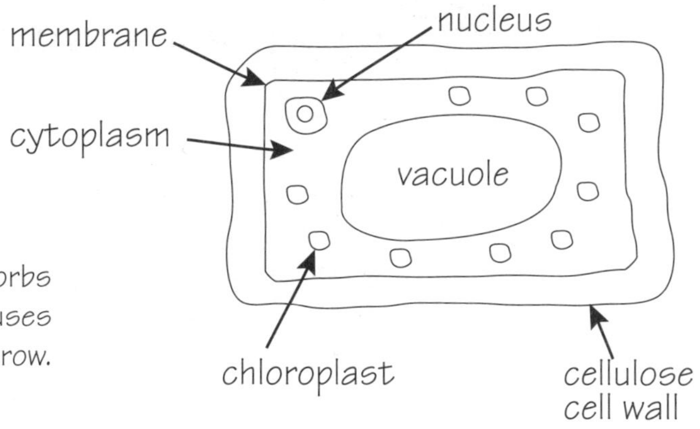

Cells, tissues, organs and systems

Most living things have many different parts – e.g. animals have muscle, blood – plants have seeds, leaves.
The cells of these different parts have features that make them specialised to do certain jobs.
Cells can form:

- **Tissues** – specialised groups of identical cells – have **same job**.
- **Organ** – many tissues grouped together – have **same job**.
- **System** – a lot of organs grouped together – have **same job**.
- **Organism** – a lot of systems grouped together.

Examples

Try to learn the names of some cells, organs, and systems.

- **Muscle tissue** – contains lots of identical muscle cells.
  Lung – organ containing different tissues – muscle + blood + nerve + other tissues.
  Respiratory system – containing different organs – lung + trachea + diaphragm + ribs and muscles.
- **Glandular tissue** – a collection of glandular cells (producing enzymes etc.).
  Stomach – organ containing different tissues – glandular + nerve + muscle + blood + other tissues.
  Digestive system – includes different organs – mouth + oesophagus + stomach + intestines + other organs.
- **Xylem tissue** – lots of xylem cells (transport water in plants).
  Leaf – an organ which contains different tissues – xylem + phloem + mesophyll + epidermis.

Life processes & cell activity

Questions

1 What is the study of plants called? ______

2 What is the study of animals called? ______

3 What is responding to changes in the environment called? ______

4 What is the release of energy from food called? ______

5 What is removing waste products from the body called? ______

6 What is removing the waste from digestion called? ______

7 What is producing new members of the species called? ______

8 What is increasing in size called? ______

9 Which gas is commonly used in respiration? ______

10 Which characteristic of living things is responsible for producing energy?

______

11 Name the seven characteristics of living things.

______

______

______

______

______

______

______

12 Which phrase helps you to remember? ______

13 What are the inside contents of a cell called? ______

14 Which part of a cell controls its functions? ______

15 What is the outside of a plant cell called? ______

16 In which part of a plant cell is chlorophyll found? ______

17 Which part of a plant cell is filled with water? ______

18 What is a group of cells with the same function called? ______

19 What is a group of tissues with one function called? ______

20 What is a group of organs working for one function called? ______

21 What do a group of organ systems make up? ______

22 What features of plant cells do animal cells not have? ______

23 What is a neurone an example of? ______

24 What is the heart an example of? ______

25 What is the stomach an example of? ______

Human as organisms

Nutrition

Humans need seven types of food in their diet:

- **carbohydrate** – e.g. **starch**, **glucose**, **sugar**, **glycogen** – used to make **energy**.
- **protein** – made from **amino acids** – used for growth and repair of cells – enzymes and some hormones are proteins.
- **fat** – made from **fatty acids** and **glycerol** – used to make energy – part of cell membranes.
- **minerals** – like **iron** – red blood cells – **lack of** = **anaemia**, and **calcium** in bones and teeth.
- **vitamins** like C – lack of = scurvy, and lack of D in bones and teeth = rickets.
- **water** – solvent for many chemicals in body.
- **fibre** – roughage – helps food travel along digestive system.

Digestion

- Carbohydrate, protein and fat are insoluble.
- **Digestion breaks down large, insoluble, complex molecules into smaller, simpler, soluble molecules**.
- **Enzymes carry out digestion** – **speed up chemical changes** – **catalysts**.

Digestive system

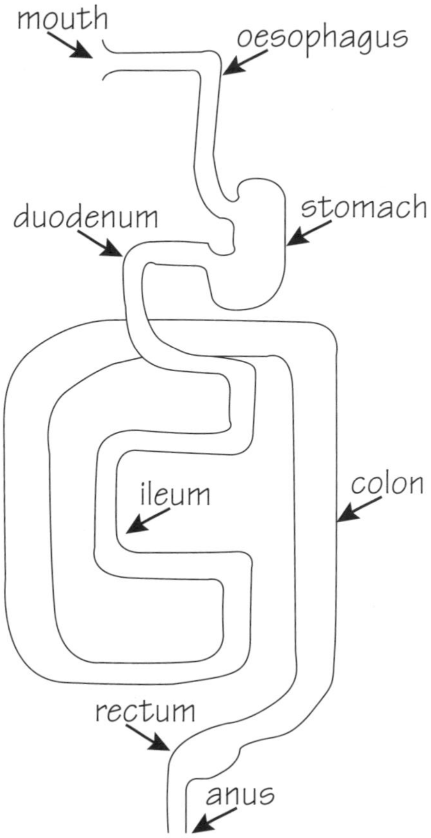

Mouth

- Chewing begins to break up food – easier to swallow.
- **Saliva** lubricates food – easier to swallow.
- Saliva contains enzyme – **carbohydrase** – starts digestion of starch to glucose.

Oesophagus

- Gullet– food squeezed – **peristalsis** – how food moves inside the gut
- produces no enzymes.

Stomach

- **Hydrochloric acid** kills germs and creates best conditions for enzymes.
- **Enzyme gastric protease** – digests protein to amino acids.

Duodenum

- **Bile** – made in the **liver** – stored in **gall bladder**.
- **Bile emulsifies fats** (breaks them into tiny droplets). **Bile is not an enzyme** – gives a large surface area for enzymes to work on.
- Bile also neutralises stomach acid.
- Digestive juice from **pancreas** – contains enzymes and neutralises acid from stomach – enzymes in duodenum need slightly alkaline conditions.
- **Lipase** – digests **fat** into **fatty acids** and **glycerol**.
- **Carbohydrase** – digests **starch** to **glucose**.
- **Proteases** – complete digestion of proteins to amino acids.

Ileum

Remember the names of the organs of the digestive system with the word MOSDICRA
Mouth
Oesophagus
Stomach
Duodenum
Ileum
Colon
Rectum
Anus

- Enzymes complete digestion – **carbohydrase**, **protease** and **lipase** digest foods as above.
- Soluble, simple food absorbed into bloodstream.
- Adapted for diffusion of small molecules – large surface area – **villi**.
- Thin, moist , semi permeable cell membranes – allow diffusion of food into blood.
- Active transport to absorb some food molecules – energy used by cells.

Note **Duodenum** + **ileum** = **small intestine**.

Large intestine – colon

- Water reabsorbed into blood – important as prevents dehydration.
- Indigestible food remains – **faeces**.

Rectum

- Stores faeces until they are eliminated through **anus**.

Circulation

Heart

Heart – simple

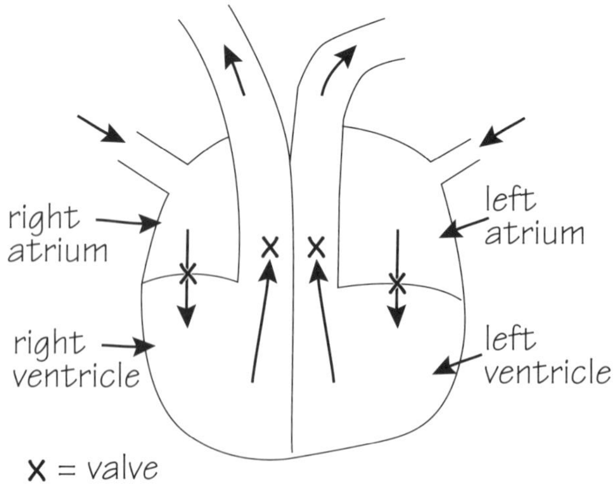

Has four chambers:
- two **atria** at top
- two **ventricles** at bottom
- **right side** pumps blood to **lungs**.
- **left side** pumps blood to **body**.
- atria contract first – then venticles.

Four valves:
- one between right atrium and ventricle.
- one between left atrium and ventricle.
- one at exit of right ventricle.
- one at exit of left ventricle.

The valves stop blood flowing in wrong direction.

Blood flow

From major vein (vena cava) ———> right atrium ———>right ventricle ———> artery ———> lungs (one circulation system) ———> vein ———> left atrium ———> left ventricle ———> artery ———> body (second circulation system).

Blood vessels

Arteries

Remember A = Artery = Away

- Thick walls – elastic – have muscle.
- Need to withstand high pressure.
- Carry blood **away** from the heart.
- Deep in the body for protection.

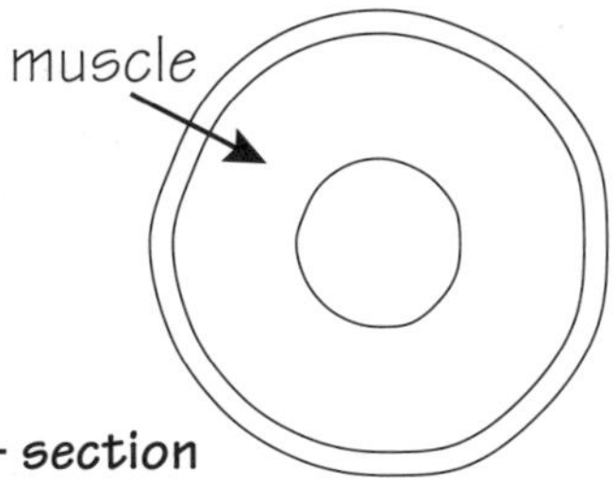

Artery – section

Veins

- Thinner walls than arteries
- Have **valves** to keep blood flowing towards heart.
- Near muscles to help squeeze blood back to heart.

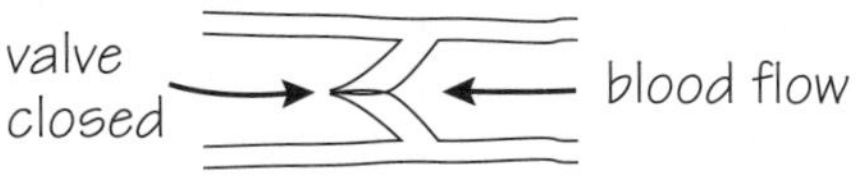

Vein

Vein = in

Capillaries

- Very thin – walls one cell thick.
- Exchange food, oxygen, carbon dioxide, waste, cell products, between blood and organs.
- Capillary exchange mechanisms in all organs, e.g. ileum, lung – alveoli, kidney – nephron.
- Provide very large surface area for diffusion.

Blood

Contains **red cells**, **white cells**, **platelets** and **plasma.**

Red Cells

- Carry **oxygen** in **haemoglobin**.
- Oxygen + haemoglobin ——————> Oxyhaemoglobin – in lungs
- Oxyhaemoglobin ——————> Oxygen + haemoglobin – in capillaries near body cells – oxygen into cells for respiration.
- No nucleus – more room to carry oxygen.
- Made in bone marrow – live approximately 120 days.
- Poisoned by **carbon monoxide** – person suffocates from lack of oxygen.

White cells

- Have nuclei.
- Made in bone marrow.
- **Immunity** – defend the body against invaders – microbes, e.g. bacteria, viruses.
- Detect invaders and ingest (eat) them.
- **Antibodies** – made by white cells – destroy microbes and foreign tissue.
- **Antitoxins** – destroy poisons produced by microbes.
- **Immune system memory** – once you have had a disease you are immune – **vaccinations** trigger immune memory – **boosters** needed as a reminder for some diseases.

Note You get lots of colds because the virus is different each time.

Platelets

- Made in bone marrow – from parts of much larger cells.
- React to cell damage / air.
- Produce fibres to trap red blood cells and **clot the blood**.

Plasma

- Liquid part of blood.
- Dissolves **carbon dioxide** – carries it to lungs.
- Carries dissolved **food from small intestine to liver** and all cells.
- Carries all cells.
- Carries **urea from liver to kidneys.**

Respiration

Breathing in
- Ribs move up and out – by muscles contracting.
- **Diaphragm** muscles contract – diaphragm moves down – flattens.
- Volume of chest increases.
- Pressure decreases (Boyle's law – physics).
- Air pressure forces air into lungs.

System includes: **trachea**, **bronchi**, **bronchioles**, **alveoli**.

Alveoli
- Air sacs – provide a large surface area for gas exchange.
- Thin – about 2 cells between air in air sac and blood.
- Moist – lined with mucus – oxygen dissolves in mucus.
- Selectively permeable membranes – allow diffusion of gases.
- Good blood supply – capillaries cover alveoli – gases **oxygen** and **carbon dioxide** exchanged.

Internal respiration – production of energy within cells.

Aerobic respiration

glucose + oxygen ————> carbon dioxide + water + energy

- Glucose carried in plasma.
- Oxygen carried in red blood cells.
- Cell cytoplasm – **mitochondria** – contains enzymes for respiration.
- Carbon dioxide carried away by plasma.
- Water – **metabolic water** – important source of water in desert animals.

Energy use
- Making molecules, e.g. proteins from amino acids.
- Muscle contraction.
- Heat production in birds and mammals – constant body temperature – homeostasis (see below).
- **Active Transport** – diffusion of small molecules against a diffusion gradient, e.g. glucose in the kidney nephron, minerals in plant roots.

Heavy exercise – still breathing – oxygen still entering muscles – aerobic respiration happens when enough oxygen present – carbon dioxide produced. Anaerobic respiration when not enough oxygen – lactic acid produced. Aerobic and anaerobic respiration can happen at same time.

Exercise
- Muscles respire **aerobically** for a short time – they rapidly run out of oxygen – **anaerobic** respiration starts.
- Glucose broken into two molecules of **lactic acid** – energy released so muscles can continue to work.
- **Lactic acid** builds up as anaerobic respiration continues.
- **Oxygen debt** results – oxygen needed to remove all lactic acid after exercise.
- Anaerobic produces much **less** energy than aerobic.
- **Carbon dioxide** is **not** produced by anaerobic respiration.

Nervous system

Central nervous system (CNS)

- Brain.
- Spinal cord.

Neurons

- Sensory – messages from receptors to CNS.
- Motor – messages from CNS to effectors, i.e. muscles, glands and organs.
- Relay – mostly in CNS – messages between sensory and motor neurons.

Stimulus ——> **receptor** ——> ***co-ordinator*** ——> **effector** ——> **response**

Eye

- **Cornea** – transparent.
- **Sclera** – tough – protection.
- **Iris** – muscles control size of **pupil** – large in dim light – small in bright light.
- **Pupil** – hole for light to enter eye.
- **Retina** – light sensitive cells.
- **Lens** – shape controlled by **suspensory ligaments** and **ciliary muscle**.
- **Optic nerve** – takes nerve impulses from retina to brain.

The eye

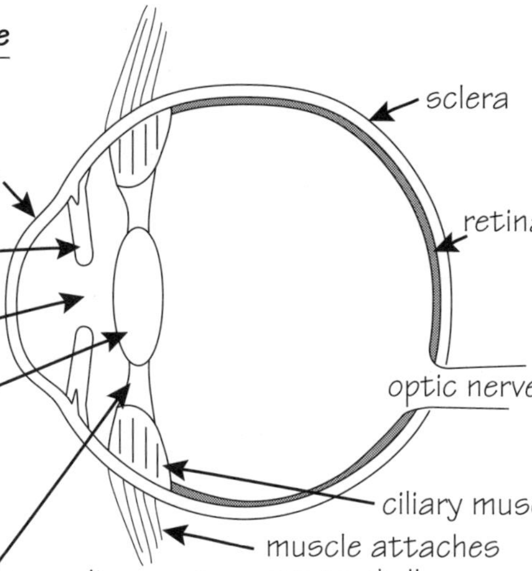

Image detection

Light enters eye ——> cornea and lens focus light on retina ——> receptor cells send message via optic nerve to brain ——> brain interprets image.

Focusing images

- Distant object – ciliary muscle relaxed – lens thin.
- Near object – ciliary muscle contracts – lens thick.

Reflect action, e.g. knee-jerk reflex

Important (You must be able to analyse any given situation in terms of **stimulus** ——> **receptor** ——> **co-ordinator** ——> **effector** ——> **response**.

- **Receptor** detects **stimulus**, e.g. tap on knee.
- Sends message (**impulse**) – sensory nerve to **CNS** – ***co-ordinator***, in this case = spinal cord.
- **Synapse** – gap between sensory neuron and relay neuron – chemical messenger crosses gap – **neurotransmitter** – passes impulse to relay neuron.
- **Synapse** – gap between relay and motor neuron – neurotransmitter – passes impulse to motor neuron.
- Motor neuron carries impulse to **effector**, in this case = thigh muscle.
- Effector produces **response**, in this case = leg moves forward.

Effectors make muscles move or glands secrete, e.g. saliva at the smell of food.

Hormones

Control and co-ordinate many body processes.

Blood sugar

Monitored and controlled by pancreas.

Glucose level in blood too high

- Pancreas releases **hormone insulin** into blood.
- Insulin picked up by **liver** from blood.
- Liver cells take glucose from blood – convert it to **glycogen** – stored.
- Blood sugar returns to normal.

Glucose level in blood too low

- **Pancreas** releases hormone **glucagon** into blood.
- **Glucagon** picked up by **liver** from blood.
- **Liver cells** convert **glycogen** to glucose – glucose released into blood.
- Blood sugar returns to normal.

Menstrual cycle

Controlled by hormones from the **pituitary gland** in the brain and the **ovaries**.

- Day 1–5 – **period** occurs.
- Days 6–13 – **uterus** lining thickens caused by **oestrogen** and **progesterone** from ovary, prepares to receive fertilised ovum – ovum maturing, caused by hormone **FSH** from pituitary.
- Day 14 – ovulation – caused by hormone **LH** from pituitary.
- Day 15–28 – embryo implants. Or not pregnant – uterus lining stops developing – lack of hormones.
- Day 29 = day 1 – uterus lining shed if not pregnant – period.

Draw a diagram like this to help you remember blood sugar control.

Menstrual cycle

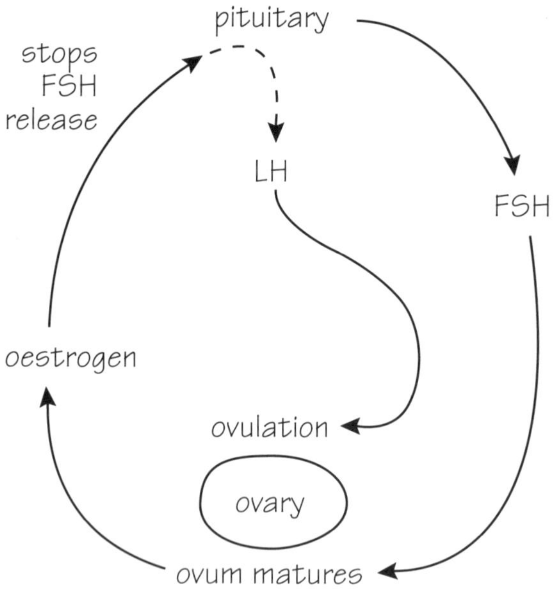

Fertility treatment

FSH given – stimulates ovum development in ovaries – more than one may mature – multiple births.

Contraception

Oestrogen given – inhibits FSH production by pituitary – no eggs mature – none released.

Problem – body thinks it's pregnant – side effects – possible weight gain, sickness, long-term effects.

Take with medical supervision only.

Water balance

Hormone – **anti-diuretic hormone** – ADH – produced by **pituitary gland**. See **Homeostasis**.

Homeostasis

Control of the body's internal environment to keep it constant.

Lungs

- Remove carbon dioxide – waste product of respiration.
- Some water lost as breath is moist.

Liver

- Excess **amino acids** broken down into **urea** + carbohydrate.
- Carbohydrate – energy source – stored as **glycogen** or used in respiration.
- **Urea** enters blood and removed by **kidneys**.

Kidneys

- Filter the blood via kidney nephron.
- All small substances removed, e.g. water, urea, salt and glucose.
- Glucose needed by body – all glucose reabsorbed by nephron by **active transport** – cells use energy to do this.
- Some salt – sodium and chloride ions – reabsorbed.
- Water – see **Osmoregulation** below.
- Urea, salt ions and water are excreted – **urine** – stored in the **bladder** – eliminated as necessary.

Osmoregulation – water regulation – most important job of kidney.

Learn this by drawing your own flow diagram!

- Brain monitors blood concentration.
- **Blood is too concentrated – not enough water.**
- Feeling of thirst – drink water.
- **Pituitary** produces **ADH** – travels in blood to kidney.
- Makes **kidney nephron more permeable** – reabsorbs water back into blood.
- **Urine is more concentrated** – less water lost.
- Blood returns to normal.

Blood too dilute – too much water

- **Pituitary** releases less **ADH**.
- **Urine more dilute** – more water lost.
- **Kidney nephron is less permeable to water**.
- Blood returns to normal.

Skin

- Sweating – loses heat, water, salt ions and some urea; temperature control

Temperature control

Thermoregulatory centre in brain monitors core body temperature.

Environment too hot

- Skin temperature **receptor** – causes impulse in sensory nerve —> brain (co-ordinator).
- Brain sends messages – nerve impulse and hormone – to blood vessels in skin – dilate (get wider) – more blood to skin surface – more heat lost.
- Also message to sweat glands – sweat on skin – liquid evaporates – cool down.

Note Capillary muscles = **effector**.
Dilating = **Response**.

Environment too cold

- Brain and skin detect.
- Message to skin blood vessels to constrict – less blood to skin – less heat lost.
- Brain –- message to muscles to shiver – produces heat by respiration.

Diseases

- Caused by **microbes** that invade body.
- Caused by toxins – poisons – produced by growing microbes.
- Growth of microbes in cells cause cell death.
- Made much worse by person being weak, e.g. in the disease AIDS.
- Usually need a lot of microbes to cause disease – unhygienic conditions, e.g. food poisoning (bacteria) – or contact with infection, e.g. chickenpox (virus).

Microbes

- Bacteria – Much smaller than animal cells – contain cytoplasm, membrane and cell wall – genes in cytoplasm, *not* in a nucleus – most bacteria are harmless and very useful, e.g. grow in soil —> nitrogen cycle – only a few cause disease.
- Antibiotics stop bacteria growing – penicillin stops cell wall production – bacteria burst and die.
- **Viruses** – much smaller than bacteria – contain protein and a few genes – can only grow inside living cells – take over cell functions – cell bursts open and dies when viruses reproduce.

Defence

- **Skin** – barrier to microbes.
- **Blood clot** – wounds quickly sealed – prevents entry of microbes.
- **Mucus** – sticky to trap microorganisms – protects nose, mouth, then lungs and stomach – open to outside.
- **Stomach** has acid – kills most microbes.
- **Immune system** – white blood cells – antibodies – see blood, circulation.

Drugs

These are any chemicals that enter the body and have an effect.
They can be:

- **useful** – e.g. paracetemol – pain relief, antibiotics – kill microbes.
- **harmful** – e.g. nicotine – dependence on cigarettes, alcohol – liver problems.
- **very dangerous** – e.g. paracetamol – can be fatal with overdose, heroin – addictive, cocaine – addictive – withdrawal problems – very hard to quit.

Drug misuse

- Effect of drugs on a person depends upon person's state of health and mind.
- Same drug can affect two different people in very different ways.

Solvents

- Seriously affect behaviour, drug is in control.
- Damage to liver, lungs and brain.
- Most deaths caused by inhaling vomit when unconscious.

Tobacco

- Nicotine is addictive – affects blood pressure – calms people down – hard to give up.
- Other chemicals in cigarettes cause cancer – throat, lung, stomach.
- Breathing problems – emphysema, bronchitis.
- Carbon monoxide, in smoke – blood carries less oxygen – high blood pressure.
- Heart and blood vessels affected – heart disease, artery disease.

Alcohol

- Affects nervous system – small amounts – mild anaesthetic – slows reactions, larger amounts – affects motor control – movement, speech – person is not in control – coma – unconsciousness can follow – can be fatal.
- Heavy drinking for a long time causes severe liver damage – sclerosis (hardening of tissue) – death will result – brain damage also.

Humans as organisms

Questions

1 Which three foods need digesting? ______

2 How does food travel along the digestive system? ______

3 What are the two functions of the acid in the stomach? ______

4 What is the function of bile? ______

5 What is the function of a protease? ______

6 Which chamber of the heart pumps blood to the lungs? ______

7 Which chamber of the heart pumps blood around the body? ______

8 Why do arteries have thick muscular walls? ______

9 Why do veins have valves? ______

10 What is the function of red blood cells? ______

11 Name three things carried by blood plasma. ______

12 Where in the lungs does diffusion take place? ______

13 Which type of respiration uses oxygen? ______

14 Which type of respiration does not use oxygen? ______

15 What is the order of events in any nervous response? ______

16 Which organs make up the CNS? ______

17 Which hormone reduces blood sugar level? ______

18 Which hormone raises blood sugar level? ______

19 Which hormone causes ova to mature? ______

20 Which hormone causes ovulation? ______

21 What happens to excess amino acids in the body? ______

22 What effect does ADH have on the kidney nephron? ______

23 What is the difference between bacteria and viruses? ______

24 What causes people to be addicted to cigarettes? ______

Green plants as organisms

Photosynthesis

- Plants **make food** by **photosynthesis**.

You must learn this equation

carbon dioxide + **water** $\xrightarrow[\text{chlorophyll}]{\text{light}}$ **glucose** + **oxygen**

- Photosynthesis controlled by **enzymes**.
- All **enzyme reaction rates are variable** depending on the conditions.

Carbon dioxide

Look up the experiments on photosynthesis! **Remember:** you test leaves for starch using iodine, you need meths to remove the green colour from the leaf first!

- **Increased carbon dioxide** – **increased photosynthesis** – only up to the point where enzymes are working as fast as they can.
- Increase in carbon dioxide after this has little effect.
- Limited light will stop an increase in carbon dioxide from having any effect.

When drawing graphs
- **Use a pencil.**
- Mark your points clearly with an X.
- Draw a line of best fit.
- Use as much of the graph paper as possible – use the largest scale you can.

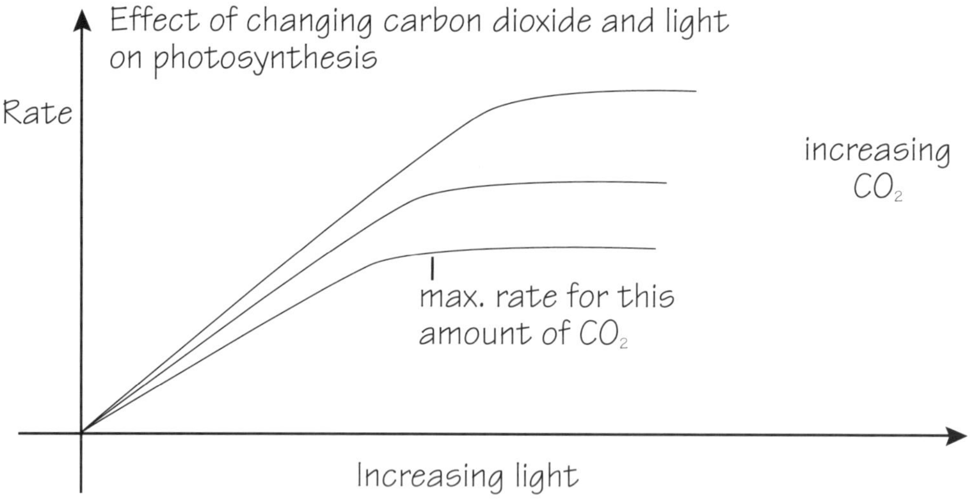

Light

- **Increased light** – **increased photosynthesis** – until enzymes are working as fast as they can.
- Increasing light after this has little effect.
- Carbon dioxide limited – will stop increase in light from having any effect.
- Low temperature stops increase in light from having any effect.
- Light absorbed by **chlorophyll** in **chloroplast**.
- Not all plant cells have chloroplasts – e.g. **epidermal** cells have a different function – protect plant.
- Specialised cells in leaf called **palisade mesophyll** – specially adapted for photosynthesis.

Temperature

- **Increased temperature** – **rate of photosynthesis increases** up to the **optimum temperature** for the enzyme.
- **Optimum temperature** – enzyme shape is a perfect fit (lock and key idea).
- Above this temperature enzyme shape starts to change – no longer fits perfectly – rate of reaction decreases – enzyme **denatures** at **high temperature**.
- Optimum temperature for photosynthesis different depending on environment plant is adapted to, e.g. desert plants adapted to higher temperatures than British plants .

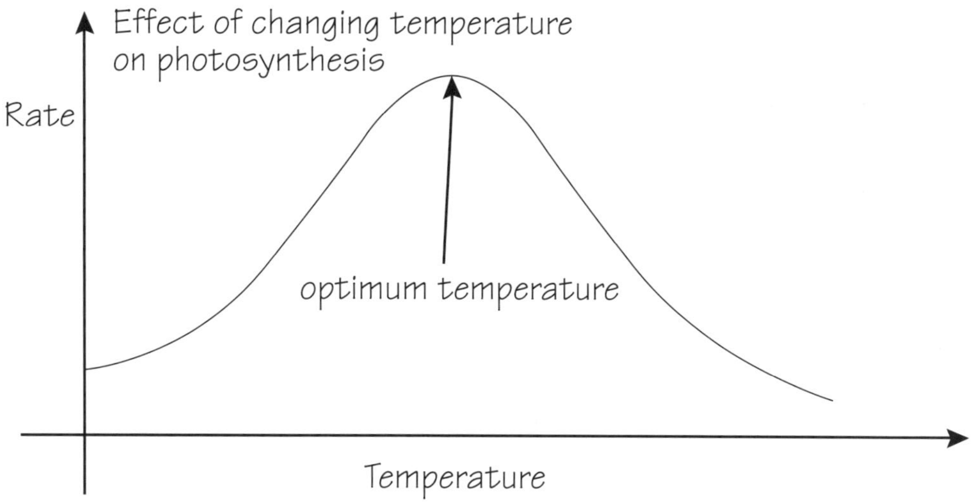

Photosynthesis and assimilation

Assimilation means **how food is used**.

In plants the sugars produced by photosynthesis are used to:

- produce **starch** – stored as a future energy/ raw material store.
- converted to **cellulose** to make cell walls.
- with **addition of nitrogen** and sometimes **phosphorus** and **sulphur** – are converted into protein.
- **proteins** are used for **growth**.
- **glucose** is used to **produce energy** needed for growth.

Plants store carbohydrate as starch and **not sugars like glucose**.

This is because:

- starch is **insoluble**.
- glucose causes large amounts of water to enter cells by osmosis – starch does not.
- Osmosis – see later section.

Transport of nutrients

- Glucose and other nutrients are transported by **phloem** cells – from leaves to:
- storage organs, e.g. roots.
- growing regions, e.g. shoot tips.
- To make essential chemicals of life plants must absorb minerals through roots.
- Different minerals have different functions in plant.

Minerals and plant health

Nitrates

- **Essential** for the **synthesis of protein**.
- Remember **glucose** contains the elements carbon, hydrogen and oxygen.
- **Proteins** contain these together with **nitrogen**.
- Protein is needed to make **membranes**, **DNA**, **enzymes** and **chlorophyll**.

Nitrate deficiency

- Causes poor growth and yellowing of leaves.
- Little protein made – no new cells as no cell membranes made, no enzymes to control cells and no chlorophyll.
- Plants try to **compensate** – produce new leaves – have to move any nitrogen they have to the growth areas – older leaves become yellow and die off.

Summary: **Plants** that are **stunted in growth** with **yellow older leaves** are **nitrate** or **nitrogen deficient**.

Potassium

- Needed for **synthesis** of **some enzymes**.
- Photosynthesis and respiration impaired – plant will have many problems.
- Cannot synthesise chemicals and produce energy.

Potassium deficiency

- Growth limited – not as badly affected as nitrate deficiency.
- Young leaves are yellow as **chlorophyll** synthesis restricted – enzyme problems.
- Leaves eventually turn green as plant moves resources to compensate areas of cell death due to lack of enzymes.

Summary: **Potassium deficiency** causes **yellow leaves with dead spots**.

Phosphate

- Needed to **synthesise some proteins** but not all.
- If essential proteins cannot be made growth will be affected.
- Phosphate has an **important role** in **photosynthesis** and **respiration**.

Phosphate deficiency

- Root growth severely affected – roots short with few side roots.
- Young leaves produced that are purple in colour.
- Chlorophyll not synthesised properly – enzyme problems.

Summary: **Phosphate deficiency** causes **stunted root growth** and **purple younger leaves**.

Plant hormones

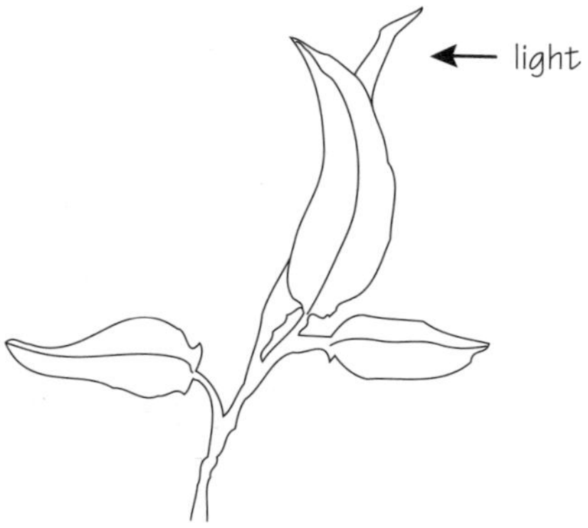

- **Hormones – control plant growth.**
- **Shoots** grow towards light – phototropism – away from gravity.
- **Roots** grow towards water and gravity – away from light.
- Shoots bend towards light because of hormone – **auxin** – causes lengthening of cells.
- Shoot tip produces auxin – this moves back down plant stem.
- Light **deactivates auxin**.
- If light from one side only – more auxin on shade side – this side lengthens more – shoot bends over **towards the light**.

Roots

- Rooting powders – used to promote growth of stem cuttings.
- Hormone promotes the growth of healthy roots on the cut stem.
- Many plants produced very quickly by promoting root growth on many stem cuttings.

Fruit

- Hormones sprayed on flowers – causes formation of fruit – fruit has not been fertilised and is seedless.
- Fruit also bigger than normal – energy has not been used to produce seeds.
- Hormones also sprayed to speed up or slow down fruit development – on the tree or after fruit picked – farmer able to produce crop at best time for climate and market.

Weedkillers

- Growth hormones sprayed onto plants – grow too quickly – run short of energy and die.
- The hormones are selective for certain types of plant – weedkiller works from within – when the plant dies the hormone should be broken down in the soil.

Benefits

You may need to discuss this in the form of a short essay!

- Production of many new plants by cuttings – identical to the parent plant.
- Development of seedless fruit.
- Selective weedkillers that do not pollute the soil.

Problems

- What if the plant hormones aren't broken down in the soil? Can enter food chain – could cause problems for other plants and animals.

Transport and water relations – transpiration

- Plants absorb most water through **root hair cells** – adapted to increase surface area for absorption.
- Plants lose water through leaves – dependent on the structure of the leaves.
- Water evaporates from spongy mesophyll cells ——> enters the spaces in leaf ——> diffuses towards the stomata pore ——> evaporates from the leaf.
- Water that is lost from the leaves is replaced by water from roots.
- **Water flows from roots through stem and to leaves in xylem vessels.**
- Movement of water called **transpiration stream** – fastest on hot, windy, dry, sunny days – slower on cold, wet and dark days.

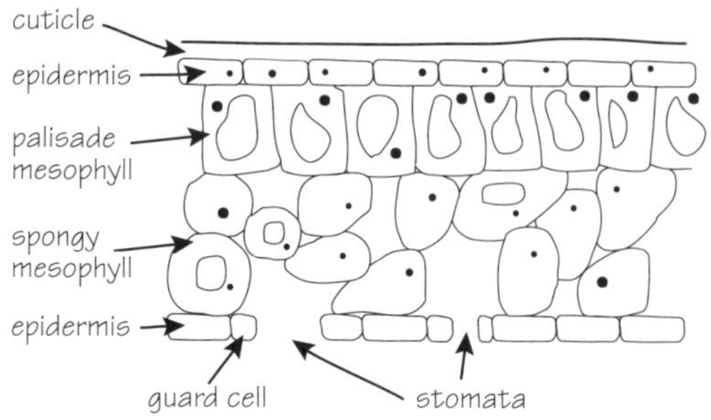

Water regulations

- **Stomata** – holes in underside of leaves – restrict the loss of water.
- Guard cells – special cells that open or close stomata.

Daylight/plant has a lot of water:
- photosynthesising as fast as possible.
- stomata wide open to allow transpiration at maximum rate.

Plant is short of water/dark:
- stomata close – restricts water loss.
- Photosynthesis also slows down or stops.

Plants that live **in dry climates** are **adapted to restrict water loss by:**
- having thicker cuticle – prevents water evaporating from upper leaf surface.
- reducing leaves to spikes, e.g. cacti.

Osmosis

Plant cells absorb or lose water by osmosis depending upon concentration of solutes

Learn your teachers' definition of osmosis

- **Gaining water** – dilute outside cell – concentrated inside – water enters cell by osmosis – cell swells.
- **Turgid** – cell full of water – turgid cells important – gives cells support.
- **Losing water** – concentrated outside cell – more dilute inside – water leaves cell by osmosis – cell shrinks.
- **Flaccid** – when only a little water is lost – plant wilts.
- **Plasmolysed** – loss of too much water – plant dies.

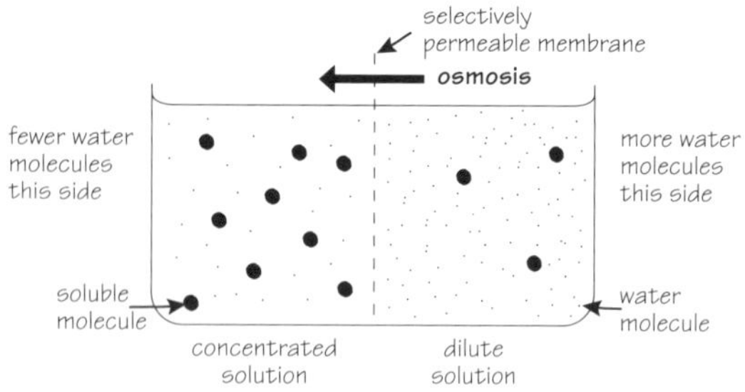

Example

Think of a plant cell as a football – the leather case is like cellulose cell wall – rubber inner tube is vacuole.

- The more air you blow into the football the harder it becomes – water entering the vacuole makes a plant cell **turgid.**
- If air is let out of the football it becomes soft – water leaving the plant vacuole makes the cell soft – **plasmolysed**.

Green plants as organisms

Questions

1 What is the green pigment in plants called and where in the cell is it found? ______

2 Which cells in the leaf are specially adapted for photosynthesis? ______

3 What is the name of the cells in a plant that transport water? ______

4 What is the name of the cells that transport food in a plant? ______

5 What is the name of the cells in a plant that transport minerals? ______

6 In which conditions would photosynthesis be greatest? ______

7 In which conditions would photosynthesis be worst? ______

8 In which conditions would transpiration be very high? ______

9 In which conditions would transpiration be very low? ______

10 Which time of year is photosynthesis greatest? ______

11 What is the name of the process that describes how glucose leaves and enters a plant cell? ______

12 By what process does water leave and enter a cell? ______

13 What word describes a cell full of water? ______

14 What word describes a cell that is lacking in water? ______

15 Which mineral deficiency causes very poor growth in plants? ______

16 Which mineral deficiency causes young leaves to be purple in plants? ______

17 Which mineral deficiency causes any leaves to turn yellow? ______

18 Which mineral deficiency causes dead spots on leaves? ______

19 Which mineral deficiency causes stunted root growth? ______

20 Which mineral deficiency causes the plant's older leaves to turn yellow? ______

21 How do plant shoots respond to light? ______

22 How do plant roots respond to gravity? ______

23 How do plant shoots respond to gravity? ______

Variation, inheritance & evolution

Causes of variation

Living things of the same species are different from each other due to two factors:

- **genes** – different living things have different genes.
- **environmental** – living things live in different environment – can affect how living things grow
  - not enough food or nutrients – animals and plants will not grow as well.
  - too much competition in one place – animals or plants may be stunted in development – opposite could also be true if there was very little competition.

Genetics

You must learn the names used in genetics

- Studying how **information** is passed on from one generation to the next.
- Information is carried in **genes** which are found on **chromosomes**.
- Different genes control different **characteristics**.
- Different forms of same gene – **alleles**, e.g. brown and blue eye colour.
- **Homozygous** – individual has both alleles of a gene the same, e.g. XX, female.
- **Heterozygous** – individual has different alleles for a gene, e.g. XY, male.
- **Dominant allele** – characteristic always develops.
- **Recessive allele** – characteristic only develops when dominant allele not present.

Chromosomes

- **Genes** are found on **chromosomes**.
- Chromosomes **in pairs** in **all body cells** of **all animals** and **plants**.
- In **humans** there are **46 chromosomes** – 23 pairs in all body cells.
- **Every cell has all genes** that carry the information to make another copy of you.
- Chromosomes made from chemical called **DNA**.
- DNA has unique property that it can duplicate itself exactly.
- When cells divide they produce exact copies of chromosomes and genes.

Heredity

- Genes are passed on from one generation to next.
- Every living thing must reproduce to survive – passing genes to next generation.
- A living thing is a biological success if it leaves copies of its genes in its offspring.
- The more copies of its genes it leaves, the bigger a success it was.

Two forms of reproductions

- **Sexual** – this mixes genes – produces much more variation in living things – evolution can happen.
- **Asexual** – produces offspring that are identical – **clones** – all **genetically same**.

Cell Division

Mitosis

Body cell division – repair and growth.

- Cells divide – produce copies of themselves – all pairs of chromosomes duplicated exactly.
- Two new cell nuclei receive identical sets of paired chromosomes.
- All body cells have identical chromosomes – there are occasional mistakes – **chromosome mutations**.

Meiosis

Production of sex cells.

- Copies of chromosomes made in **testes of males** after puberty – in **ovaries of females** before they are born – in **ovaries** and **anthers** of **plants**.
- Pairs of chromosomes separated.
- Cell divides to form four sex cells – each cell only has one copy of the chromosome.

Human genetics

- Human cells have 46 chromosomes in nuclei.
- When ovum fertilised to produce baby, baby must also have 46 chromosomes.
- Sex cells – sperm and ova – have 23 chromosomes.
- Sperm and ovum contribute equally to embryo.
- 23 chromosomes from sperm + 23 chromosomes from ovum = 46 chromosome embryo.

Inheritance of sex

- Humans have sex chromosomes called X and Y.
- Females have two X chromosomes (XX).
- Males have one X and one Y (XY).
- When sex cells produced – sex chromosomes separate and end up in different cells.
- All ova have X chromosome only.
- Two types of sperm – one with Y chromosome – one with X chromosome.

mother	XX	×	XY father
ovum	X		X or Y sperm
offspring	XX girl		XY boy

Cystic fibrosis

- Caused by **recessive gene**.
- Breathing and digestion problems – membranes do not secrete normally.
- Sufferers have a short life expectancy.
- Adults can be normal but carry a recessive cystic gene – **carrier**.
- Condition usually runs in families but may miss generations.

Let N = normal dominant gene and c = recessive cystic gene.

parents	(Nc)	×	(Nc)
sex cells	N or c		N or c
offspring	1 NN normal 25% chance	:2 Nc carrier 50% chance	:1 cc cystic fibrosis 25% chance

	N	c
N	NN	Nc
c	Nc	cc

Conclusion: Two carrier parents have a 25% chance of having a cystic child.

Huntington's chorea

- Caused by a **dominant gene**.
- Affects the nervous system – loss of motor and sensory function – quickly leads to death.
- Person will be perfectly normal until about 35 to 45 years of age – develop Huntington's chorea – become seriously ill and die.
- By this time may have had their family and passed the gene on to children.

Sickle cell anaemia

- Caused by **recessive gene**.
- Disease is inherited from both parents who carry the gene.
- Name comes from shape of the red blood cells that disease produces.
- **Sickle cell disease** is **fatal**.
- Gene is still in populations of people who live where there is **malaria** – carriers of the gene have a greater resistance to malaria than normal people.
- So in malaria areas – NN catch malaria and die – Ns survive – ss die of sickle cell anaemia.

Structure of DNA

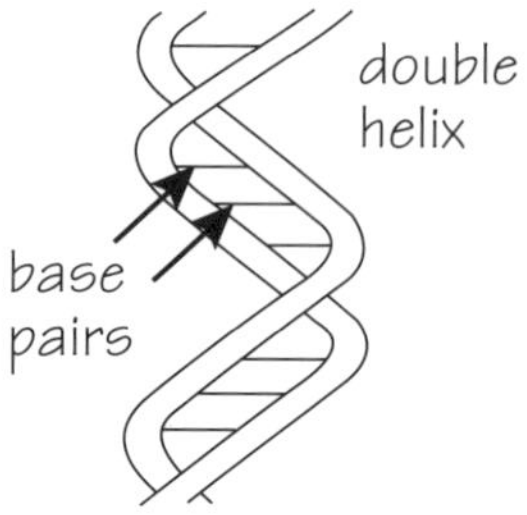

- Two long strands that coil around each other – form **double helix** shape.
- Strands linked together by **hydrogen bonds** – from one **base** to another.
- 4 bases (chemicals) in DNA – called A, T, C, and G.

DNA is able to replicate itself exactly.

- Double helix 'unzips' – each side acts as a template to build another DNA strand.
- Result is **two** double helixes of DNA.
- These separate into new cells as cell cytoplasm divides.
- Happens to **all** chromosomes (strands of DNA) at same time so the division of cells is co-ordinated.

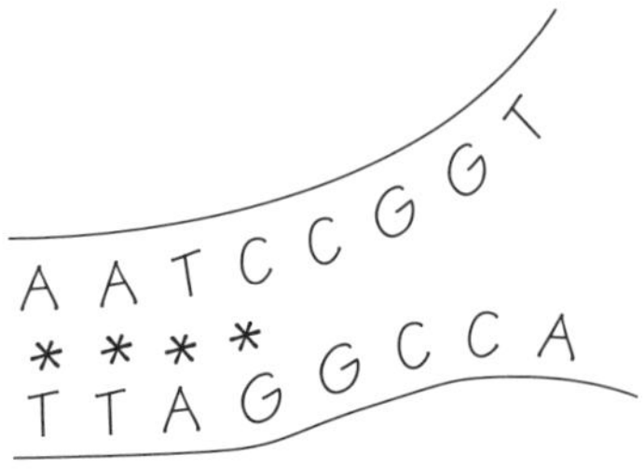

* = hydrogen bond

Protein synthesis

- Order of bases of DNA very important.
- Order codes for all proteins.
- Three nucleic acid bases code for one amino acid.

gene on DNA – copied to single strand of messenger RNA – **mRNA**

→ mRNA leaves nucleus – goes to **ribosome** in cytoplasm

→ ribosome **transcribes** mRNA into protein – amino acids lined up one at a time along mRNA – protein made

→ ribosome finishes protein – mRNA either destroyed or used again to make another copy of same protein

→ protein leaves ribosome – cell uses the protein or exports for use in another part of body, e.g. digestive enzymes or hormones

Mutation

- Change in gene code – DNA instructions changed.
- Gene mutations when ova and sperm being produced will be passed on to offspring – embryo will not survive if mutation too great.
- Only small mutations passed on this way, e.g. Down's syndrome.
- Down's syndrome – one sex cell (usually ovum) contains one extra chromosome – the embryo has 47 chromosomes instead of 46 – affects development – produces child with symptoms of Down's syndrome.

Chromosome changes in adults

- Cells divide and produce new cells – making new chromosomes can go wrong.
- **Mutations** can occur naturally with a mistake in replication of DNA.
- Dead cell is destroyed by immune system and no harm results.
- Some mutations caused by **ionising radiation**, e.g. ultra violet, gamma rays, X-rays.
- Also caused by chemicals such as tar from cigarettes.
- Greater exposure – more mutations – greater chance that cell survives – cell will replicate – pass mutation on to daughter cells.
- This mutation remains in the one organism unless is where sex cells are made.
- Workers with radiation must be shielded and protected – e.g. lead jackets and shielded cubicles of Radiographers, test badges of nuclear power workers.
- **Cancer** – cells lose ability to stop dividing – **grow out of control**.

Genetic engineering

When genes are artificially transferred from one living thing to another – between members of same or different species .

Benefits

Conquering cystic fibrosis.

- Healthy gene could be placed into cell in embryo.
- Would divide and provide the embryo with normal secretions in lungs.
  Or
- Same gene could be transferred via virus directly into the lungs of cystic child.
- Virus genetically engineered to carry healthy gene – infects lungs of child – healthy gene transferred and starts to work in child.

Producing human insulin.

- Insulin gene inserted into a bacterial cell.
- Bacteria can be cultured – produce human protein coded by gene.
- Insulin collected, purified and used by diabetics.

Disadvantages

- How far do scientists go?
- Do we clone human beings?
- Do we select the genes of our children?
  The moral debate will continue.

Tissue culture

A small group of cells taken from a plant or animal – grown using special media and chemicals such as hormones.

Advantages

Be prepared to write a short essay to discuss advantages and disadvantages of genetic engineering

- Can produce thousands of identical plants from one small tissue culture.
- All plants genetically identical – **clones.**
- Human or animal cells also grown as tissue cultures – they don't form living things, just sheets of cells – can be used to test drugs etc. – saves using live animals.
- **Embryo transplants** carried out this way – fertilised ovum produces ball of cells – split up – each cell develops into an embryo on its own – vets use technique if farmer wants to produce lots of identical offspring in cattle, pigs or sheep.

Cloning

This is not quite genetic engineering – not altering genes – manipulating cells or cell nuclei – technique used in both plants and animals.

Problems

Be prepared to write a short essay on benefits and problems

- Moral questions about human use of cultured embryos.
- Genes in clones all same – can cause problems..
- Lack of variation – evolutionary process has been stopped.
- Wild herds must be kept alive to maintain large number of natural genes for future generations to breed from.

Selective breeding

- Humans use knowledge of genetics to select which animals and plants to breed.
- Right choice animals to breed from could improve herd, e.g.
  – herds of cows that produce more milk
  – pigs that grow bigger
  – disease resistant cereals.

Evolution

- Evidence comes from **fossils** – found in rocks.
- Fossils show us how living things have changed – or stayed same – over millions of years.

Formation of fossils

- Hard parts of animals and plants – do not decay easily – covered by sand/silt – replaced over millions of years by minerals in rocks – animal/plant becomes rock – **fossil**.
- Sometimes soft tissues do not decay – reason? – microbes that cause matter to decay are absent or no oxygen to help decay process etc. – soft tissue then makes fossil.
- Life evolved over 3000 million years ago.
- Living things today evolved from living things from past – life evolved from first simple living things.
- Evolution takes millions of years – many animals and plants have become **extinct**.
- Changes in living things in fossil record – evidence that supports theory of evolution.

Natural selection

How evolution happens.

- One species of living thing has many individual differences – differences are passed on in parents' genes – from generation to generation by reproduction.

Process of natural selection

- One characteristic very well suited to environment.
- May give that animal or plant and its offspring an advantage.
- Advantage (e.g. camouflage in an insect) means that animal survives – passes on its genes to its offspring.
- Over many generations camouflage may get better and species changes colour or shape – **evolution**.
- Characteristics suited to environment are passed on from one generation to next.
- Living things that 'fit' their environment will survive, those less well adapted could become extinct.

Variation, inheritance & evolution
Questions

1 How many chromosomes are in a human cell nucleus? ____________________

2 What do you call the 'packages' of information on chromosomes? __________

3 What chemical are chromosomes made from? ____________________

4 How many chromosomes are there in a human sperm cell? ________________

5 How many chromosomes are there in a human ovum? __________________

6 What is the chromosome pair for sex determination in a human male? ________

7 What is the chromosome pair for sex determination in a human female? ______

8 Which word describes species of living things which no longer exist? _________

Use the words below to describe the following pairs of genes for questions 9 to 13.

A homozygous recessive, B homozygous dominant, C heterozygous

9 The genotype XX ________________

10 The genotype XY ________________

If B = brown eyes and is dominant, b = blue eyes and is recessive

11 Bb __________

12 BB __________

13 bb __________

14 What gives us the most information about evolution? ____________________

15 By what process does evolution occur? ____________________

16 How long ago did life evolve on Earth? ____________________

17 What are genetically identical living things called ? ____________________

18 What is the name of the process where humans control the breeding of animals? ____________________

19 What is the process of body cell division called? ____________________

20 What is the process of sex cell division called? ____________________

21 What do we call the process where genes are transferred from one living thing to another? ____________________

22 Which types of radiation cause mutations? ____________________

____

Living things & their environment

Adaptation & competition

- **Living things live where conditions suit them.**
- **They are in competition with each other.**
- **Population** – group of animals or plants of same species living in same place.
- **Community** – group of populations of different species living in same place, e.g. pond, wood.

Population size

Population size may be affected by **competition** for/with:

- **food** – animals and plants compete for food resources – if successful, will survive to breed.
- **space and light** – plants – photosynthesis needs light
  – animals – **carnivore** needs area to live in with enough **prey** animals for food – will often defend this area as its **territory** and drive away any other predators.
- **living things** – herbivores restrict the growth and populations of plants
  – carnivores restrict populations of herbivores and other carnivores.
- **humans** – can remove or introduce species – can affect whole food chain – effect may be devastating, e.g. grey squirrel vs. red squirrel.
- **disease** – may deplete a population, e.g. myxomatosis kills rabbits .

Human impact on the environment

Air pollution

- **Sulphur dioxide** and **nitrogen oxides**.
- Produced when fossil fuels are burnt in furnaces and engines.
- These gases are dangerous – can cause asthma attacks.
- Gases dissolve in rain water to produce **acid rain**.
- This can kill plants – if acid content of rivers and lakes becomes too high, animals and plants cannot survive.

Increasing human population

- Raw materials – **resources** of Earth are being rapidly used up.
- Many resources are **non-renewable**.
- Greater standard of living – resources used faster.
- Leads to more waste – can lead to greater pollution unless there are adequate controls.

Management of Earth's resources and waste produced is one of the biggest problems to solve in the 21st century.

Water pollution

Polluted water can interfere with all of life's processes.

Pollutants

- Factory waste – may include **acid**, **cyanide** or metals such as **mercury** and **lead**.
- Acid irritates cells – damages plant roots – fish gills – prevents diffusion of oxygen – kills fish.
- Cyanide – poison of respiratory system – prevents cells from making energy – can kill in seconds – enters food chain.
- Mercury and lead **affect bone** and **nerve cells.**

Fertilisers

- Sprayed onto fields to increase crop production.
- Minerals are soluble – get washed away into rivers and lakes.
- Fertilisers increase growth of **algae** in water.
- Water turns green with algae in badly affected lake.
- Algae absorb light – stops it from reaching plants below surface.
- Bottom living plants will die.
- Dead plants decomposed by bacteria – uses oxygen from water.
- Water depleted in oxygen – animals suffocate and die.
- Bottom living plants also hold mud with their roots – when they die a lot of mud and silt may be washed down to sea.
- River banks may collapse.
- Whole ecosystem of river or lake may be damaged.

Water becoming deoxygenated by decomposition of dead matter is called eutrophication. **Polluting water** with **untreated sewage** has the **same effect**.

Deforestation

- **Plants absorb carbon dioxide during photosynthesis.**
- **Release carbon dioxide** CO_2 during **respiration** – **absorb more than they give out**.
- Large numbers destroyed – level of CO_2 in air will increase.
- Wood is often burnt – releases more CO_2.
- Tropical rainforests contain enormous number of plants – are being destroyed at an alarming rate.
- Could mean more CO_2 remains in atmosphere.
- Could cause **increased greenhouse effect** – increase in temperature.

Greenhouse effect

- Earth is warm – has insulating layer – this traps some heat from Sun – prevents it from being re-radiated back into space – **greenhouse effect**.
- Water and carbon dioxide part of layer – absorb heat and radiate it back to Earth's surface.
- Has enabled life on Earth to survive.
- Recently has been giving cause for concern.
- Atmosphere has 0.03%. of carbon dioxide – level, increasing over recent years – increased burning of fossil fuels – destruction of the tropical rainforests.
- Estimated that doubling CO_2 levels – rise in temperature of 2 °C.
- Other gases trap heat as well – methane, some chlorofluorocarbons and nitrous oxides.
- Methane produced in intestines of cattle – also produced by rice plants as they grow.
- Producing more rice and beef or milk – increasing levels of methane in atmosphere – adding to greenhouse effect.

Weigh up the evidence and form your own opinions. Be prepared to discuss it!

Increasing temperature may mean:
- changes in weather – problems with food production.
- rise in sea level – problems in coastal areas for all living things – loss of environment.

Use of ecosystems

Be prepared to write a short essay on managing food production

- Organisms used by humans for food – crops grown.
  – animals kept on farms and fish caught in sea.
- Stocks of wild animals used for food can be depleted, e.g. fishing – control number and size of fish caught – no control – fish population may crash – valuable food source lost for many years.

Careful management of natural stocks is needed and this may be achieved by governments co-operating to:

- agreeing quotas or limits on number of animals removed from wild each year.
- being selective in which animals taken, e.g. only take non breeding adult animals, not young or breeding animals.
- avoid animal's breeding season – do not use breeding areas for fishing or hunting.

Artificial ecosystems

Those created by humans – amount of food produced in these areas kept very high by:

- using fertilisers.
- using pesticides and fungicides to destroy pests.
- reducing competition with wild animals and plants by various means.
- bringing extra water by irrigation channels from reservoirs.
- selectively breeding better animals and plants that are disease-resistant or grow bigger or faster.
- using genetic engineering to produce disease-resistant crops.

Can have major effect on natural ecosystems – natural world needs consideration before farmland created.
All domestic animals need to be treated in humane way while growing, being transported and when killed.

Efficient artificial ecosystems

- Using short food chains – short food chain less energy lost between links in chain.
- Food animals lose energy when move around – if movement restricted animals will grow faster – reason behind factory farming. Is it humane? Is it necessary?
- Controlling temperature – heating areas reduces heat lost by animals.

Energy & nutrient transfer

Producers

Sun is source of energy for all life on Earth.

- Green plants – capture the energy from Sun.
- Store energy in cells.
- Some energy used – growth and repair, making protein, fat etc.
- Some lost as waste.

Consumers

- Animals – some eat plants, some eat animals.
- Energy of plant or animal taken in.
- Energy used for repair, growth, making proteins, e.g. hormones, enzymes.
- Respiration produces energy for living processes.
- Energy lost in faeces – also as waste from chemical reactions in cells.
- Energy lost as heat – animals produce heat as they move – heat energy lost to air.
- **Mammals** and **birds** lose more energy this way – **warm blooded** – **homoiothermic**.

Decomposers

- Microbes – bacteria and fungi.
- Dead materials completely decomposed – all energy originally captured by plant back into environment.

Pollution enters food chain e.g.

- **mercury** builds up in plant tissue.
- fish eat plants – mercury in diet.
- mercury level builds up in fish – may kill fish.
- fish eaten by predator, e.g. otter or pike.
- these top consumers get high doses of Mercury in diet – eventually kills them.

Often top consumer dies – levels of poison may not be high enough in producer or primary consumer – level increases further along the food chain you go – often reaches lethal levels at final predator.

Food webs e.g.

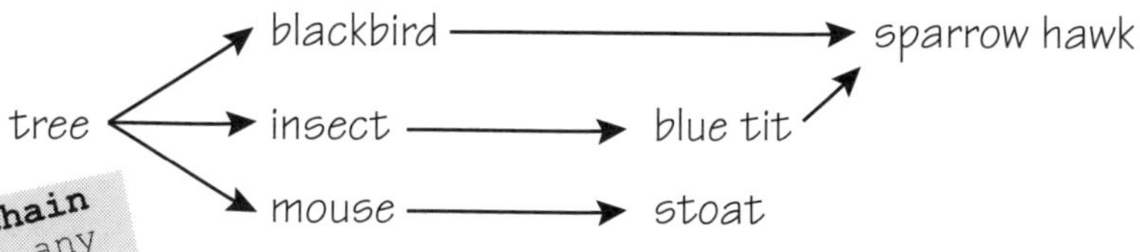

A **food chain** would be any single line from producer to top consumer

Pyramid of numbers

You will need to know how to construct pyramids properly

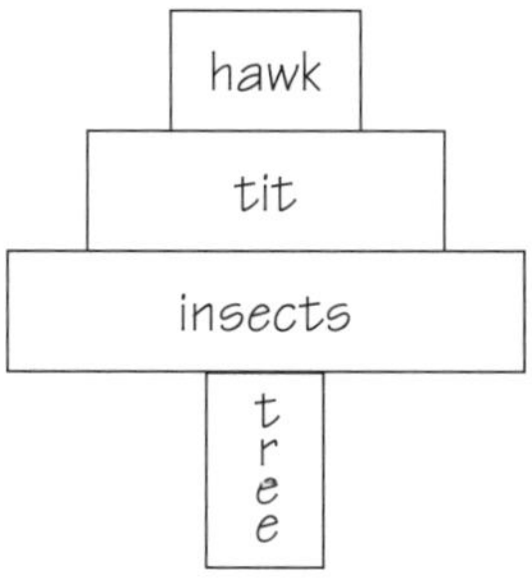

A large tree has a strange number pyramid – there is only one living thing at the base – not millions

Pyramid of biomass

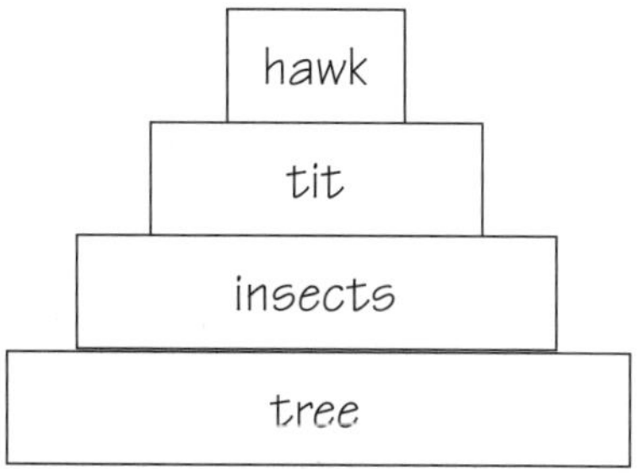

The size of each box in a pyramid representing the number of individuals or amount of biomass at that level

Carbon cycle

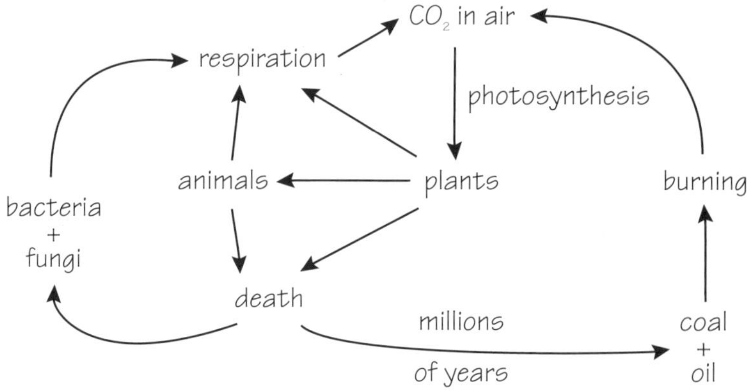

- **Carbon** in **carbohydrate**, **protein** and **fat**.
- Plants get their carbon from air – carbon dioxide (CO_2).
- Use it to make food – photosynthesis – build proteins, fats and carbohydrates.
- Animals get carbon by eating plants and other animals.
- Respiration – uses food – releases carbon dioxide back into air.
- Plants **take in** carbon dioxide – animals give out carbon dioxide.
- Plants and animals die – bodies decompose.
- Dead matter broken down by bacteria and other microbes – decomposers – carbon into their bodies.
- Decomposers also respire – carbon dioxide into air.
- Burning – releases carbon dioxide into air – extra carbon dioxide.

Nitrogen cycle

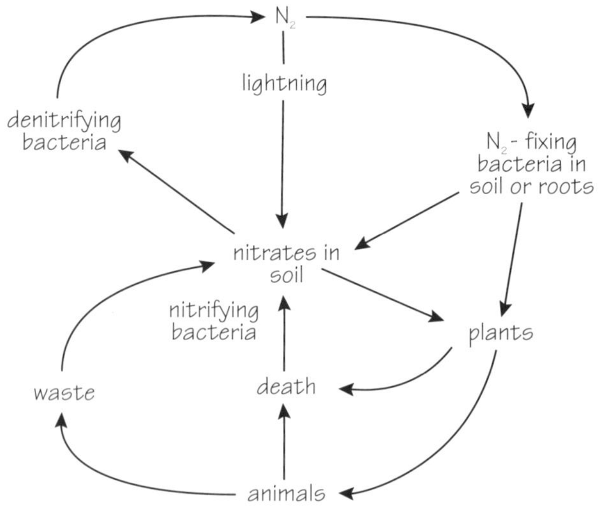

- Nitrogen (N_2) needed to make **proteins**.
- Proteins build animal and plant tissue.
- Plants build proteins – take **nitrate** out of soil through roots.
- Animals eat plants – break down plant protein – build up animal protein.
- Animals excrete **urea and faeces** – contains nitrogen waste.
- Animals and plants die – the nitrogen can be returned to the cycle.
- Decomposing bacteria break the protein / urea / faeces down into ammonia (nitrogen + hydrogen).
- **Nitrifying bacteria** change this ammonia to nitrate (nitrogen + oxygen).
- Plant roots absorb nitrate – cycle again.
- **Denitrifying bacteria** – change nitrate into nitrogen gas.
- **Nitrogen fixing bacteria** – take nitrogen out of air – build it into nitrates. These bacteria can be found by themselves in soil, or living in roots of plants belonging to pea and bean family, e.g. clover, peas etc. These plants are called **legumes**.

Living things & their environment

Questions

1 What is contained in fertiliser that seriously pollutes rivers? ________

2 Why do living things need carbon? ________

3 Why do living things need Nitrogen? ________

4 Where do most plants get their nitrogen? ________

5 Where do herbivores get their nitrogen for amino acids? ________

6 Where do carnivores get their nitrogen? ________

7 What is the name of the microbes that change nitrate into nitrogen gas? ________

8 What is the name of the microbes that change nitrogen gas into nitrate? ________

9 What is the end product of urine breakdown by nitrifying bacteria? ________

10 Which raw materials are used by plants to make amino acids during photosynthesis? ________

11 Where do plants get their carbon from? ________

12 Where do animals get their carbon from? ________

13 What is the waste product of plant respiration? ________

14 What is the waste product of animal respiration? ________

15 What percentage of the air is carbon dioxide? ________

16 Which type of microbes live in the root nodules of legumes? ________

17 Which gas is mainly responsible for destructive 'acid rain'? ________

18 Which gases are responsible for the 'greenhouse effect'? ________

19 Rain is often naturally slightly acid. Which gas is responsible for 'natural' acid rain? ________

20 Which gases are the major pollutants from coal fired power stations? ________

21 Which pollutant will damage the gills of fish? ________

22 Which poison prevents cells from making energy? ________

23 Which heavy metal has been linked to nerve damage in inner city school children? ________

24 Which heavy metal can make bones very brittle as well as causing nerve damage? ________

Life processes & living things • Answers

Life processes and cell activity

1 Botany 2 Zoology 3 Sensitivity 4 Respiration 5 Excretion 6 Elimination or egestion 7 Reproduction 8 Growth 9 Oxygen 10 Respiration 11 Movement – respiration – sensitivity – feeding – excretion – reproduction – growth 12 MRSFERG 13 Cytoplasm 14 Nucleus 15 Cellulose cell wall 16 Chloroplast 17 Vacuole 18 Tissue 19 Organ 20 System 21 Organism 22 Vacuole – cellulose – chlorophyll 23 Cell 24 Organ 25 Organ

Humans as organisms

1 Carbohydrate, protein, fat 2 Peristalsis
3 Kills germs and creates best conditions for enzymes to work.
4 Emulsifies fats – increases surface area of fat globules for enzymes to work on.
5 Digests protein 6 Right ventricle 7 Left ventricle
8 Withstand high blood pressure 9 Keep blood travelling the right way – prevent backflow 10 Carry oxygen 11 Urea, carbon dioxide, any food, hormones 12 Walls of alveoli 13 Aerobic 14 Anaerobic 15 Stimulus—>receptor —>coordinator—>effector—>response 16 Brain and spinal cord 17 Insulin 18 Glucagon 19 FSH 20 LH 21 Broken down to urea by liver 22 More permeable to water – water reabsorbed back into blood – concentrated urine produced 23 Bacteria – larger – more genes – can survive on their own. Viruses – much smaller – few genes + protein – only grow inside living cells
24 Nicotine

Green plants as organisms

1 Chlorophyll – in chloroplasts 2 Palisade mesophyll 3 Xylem 4 Phloem 5 Xylem 6 Bright light 7 Dark/cloudy 8 Warm/windy 9 Cold/wet/still 10 Summer 11 Diffusion 12 Osmosis 13 Turgid 14 Plasmolysed 15 Nitrate 16 Phosphate 17 Potassium 18 Potassium 19 Phosphate 20 Nitrate 21 Grow towards 22 Grow towards 23 Grow away

Variation, inheritance & evolution

1 46 2 Genes 3 DNA 4 23 5 23 6 XY 7 XX 8 Extinct
9 Homozygous recessive 10 Heterozygous 11 Heterozygous
12 Homozygous dominant 13 Homozygous recessive 14 Fossils 15 Natural selection 16 Over 3000 million 17 Clones 18 Selective breeding 19 Mitosis 20 Meiosis 21 Genetic engineering 22 Ultra-violet, X-ray, gamma

Living things & their environment

1 Nitrate/phosphate 2 'building brick' of all molecules of life 3 To make proteins 4 Nitrate 5 Plants 6 Other animals 7 Denitrifiers 8 Nitrogen fixers 9 Ammonia 10 Nitrate, carbon dioxide, water 11 Carbon dioxide 12 Plants 13 Carbon dioxide 14 Carbon dioxide 15 0.03% 16 Nitrogen fixers 17 Sulphur dioxide 18 Carbon dioxide and methane 19 Carbon dioxide 20 Sulphur dioxide and nitrogen oxides 21 Sulphur dioxide as acid rain 22 Cyanide 23 Lead 24 Mercury

Materials & their Properties

Classifying materials

Atomic structure

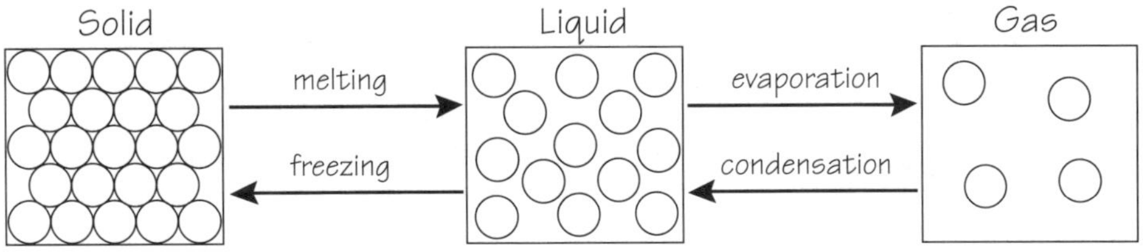

Evaporation occurs at any temperature
Boiling occurs at the **boiling point** of a liquid and depends on pressure

- **Solids – fixed shape – particles vibrate but cannot move about freely – strong forces of attraction between particles.**
- **Liquid – take shape of container – particles free to move within liquid – weaker forces of attraction between particles.**
- ***Gases* – fill container – particles free to move anywhere – no forces of attraction.**

Change of state

Solid → liquid → gas – heat energy makes particles vibrate more violently → forces become weaker → particles separate → free to move about.

- **Nucleus** has **protons** and **neutrons** – surrounded by **shells** containing **electrons**.

( ) = **maximum** number of **electrons**

Complete a shell before starting a new one

NB Only electrons can change

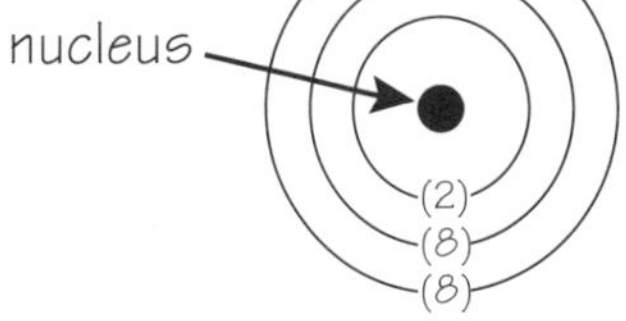

Shells fill from the **inside first**

- Relative **charges** and **masses** of neutrons (**n**), protons (**p**) and electrons (**e**):

	Mass	Charge
p	1	+1
n	1	0
e	negligible	-1

p and e **different** in **ions**

- **Neutral atom** – number of protons **equals** number of electrons.
- **Atomic number (proton number)** – number of protons in nucleus – also **name/position** of element.
- **Mass number** – number of neutrons and protons **added** together.

Atoms represented by:

symbol e.g. $^{23}_{11}$Na p = 11, n = 12 (23 - 11), e = 11

electron arrangement 2, 8, 1

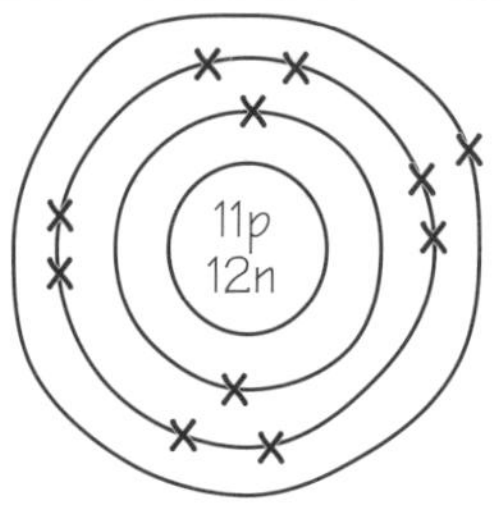

- Electrons in **outermost shell** is the group number (Na is **group 1**).
- Electrons in outer shell determine **reactivity** and **type** of reaction – metals lose electrons → positive ions.
  – non-metals gain electrons → negative ions or share electrons with other atoms.
- **Isotopes** – same atomic number but **different** mass number – **same** number of protons, **different** number of neutrons.

e.g. $^{35}_{17}$Cl (p = 17, **n** = **18**) $^{37}_{17}$Cl (p = 17, **n** = **20**)

Same chemical properties

Bonding

- Atoms more stable when outer shell full – gain, lose or share electrons until outer shell full.
- Atoms combine by **bonding** to form new substances.

An **ion** is a **charged** atom

Two types bond:

Covalent
- between **non-metals**
- electrons **shared**
- **dot and cross** diagram

e.g. methane (CH_4)

Only need to draw **outer** shells when showing bonding

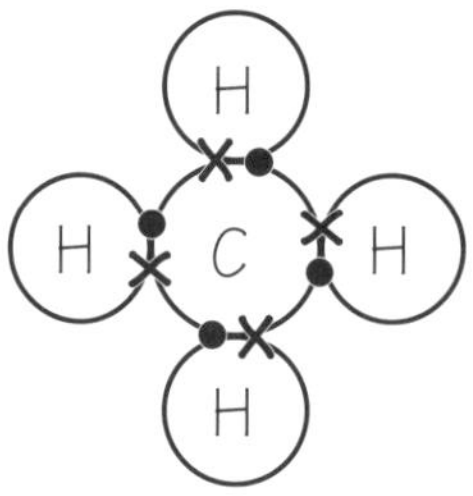

x = C electron o = H electron
C in group 4 (4e in outer shell)

Ionic
- between metal and **non-metal**
- electrons **transferred**

e.g. sodium chloride (NaCl)

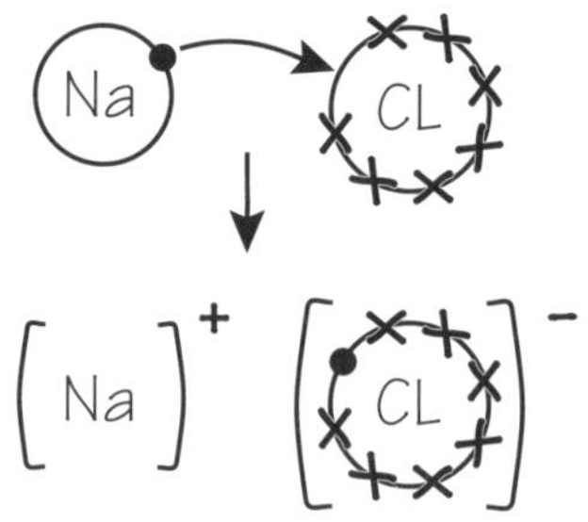

Na loses 1 electron charge **+ 1** as 1 **more p than e**

Cl **gains** 1 electron charge **- 1** as 1 **more e than p**

- Bonding causes atoms to become **more stable** by achieving the electron arrangement of a **noble gas**.
- **Properties of compounds** related to **strengths** of attractions **between** particles.
- **Giant ionic – strong** electrostatic attractions in **lattice** – lead to high melting point (m.pt) and high boiling point (b.pt).

e.g. NaCl

Noble gases have full outer electron shells e.g. He 2 Ne 2, 8 Ar 2, 8, 8

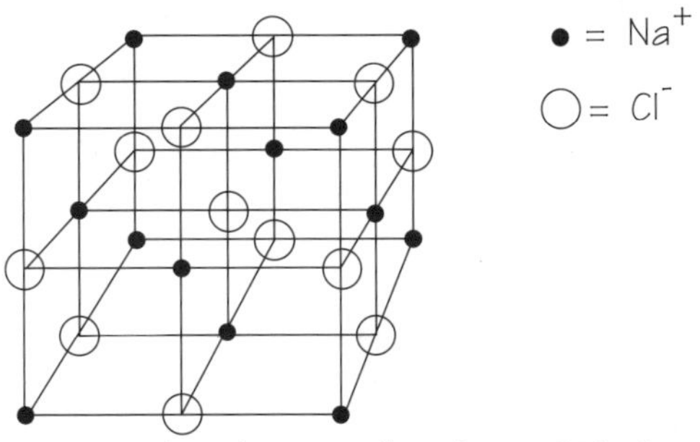

- **Covalent** – can be **giant molecular** – SiO_2 (sand), graphite, diamond – large number of bonds in structure.
  – or **simple molecular** – NH_3 H_2O.
- Graphite – layered structure → weak forces between layers → layers can slide → lubricant → each C forms 3 covalent bonds → mobile electrons → electrical conduction.

- Diamond – each C forms 4 bonds → rigid structure.
- No mobile electrons → no electrical conduction.

All electrons form covalent bonds. None are mobile

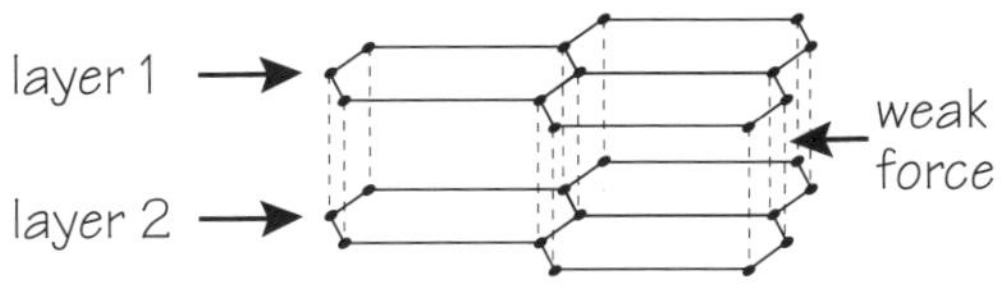

graphite

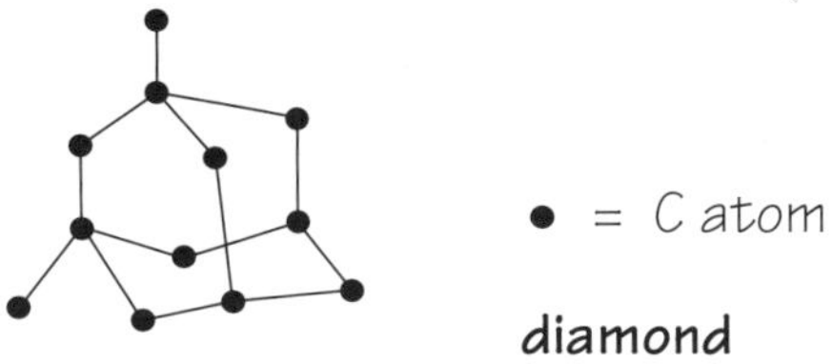

diamond

- Diamond – each C forms 4 bonds → rigid structure.
- No mobile electrons → no electrical conduction.

Properties

Property	Giant ionic	Giant molecular	Simple molecular
m.pt/b.pt	high	high	low
states	solid	solid	solid, liquid or gas
solubility in water	good	poor	poor
solubility in organic solvent	poor	poor	good
electrical conduction (**molten/aqueous** only) (**except graphite**)	yes	no	no

- NB **Strong** covalent bonds **between atoms** but **weak** attractions **between molecules** in molecular substances lead to low m.pt and b.pt.

Metallic bonding

Positive ions in a sea of electrons – more delocalised mobile electrons → stronger bonding.

- Outer shell electron of metal atom – free to move through structure – allows metals to conduct heat and electricity.
- Electrons hold atoms in a very strong regular structure.
- High melting/boiling points.
- Atoms slide over each other → malleable and ductile

e.g. structure of sodium

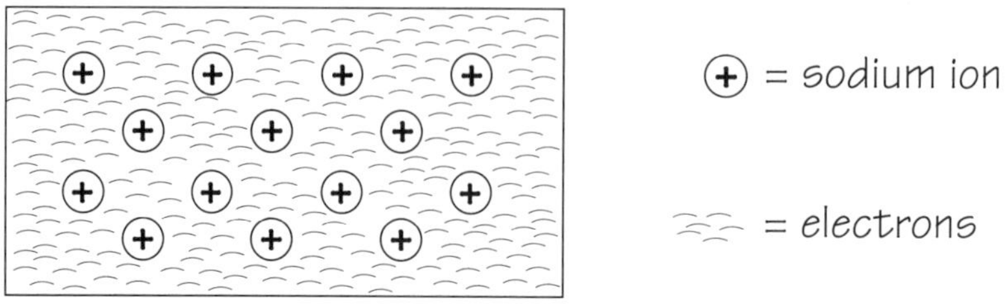

Alloys

- Usually **mixture** of metals.
- Different size atoms prevent slip → hard metals.
- Less dense – more space between atoms created by large atom.

- e.g. (a) steel: iron, carbon, nickel, manganese, chromium.
  (b) dental filling: mercury, silver, iron.

Be able to recognise alloys

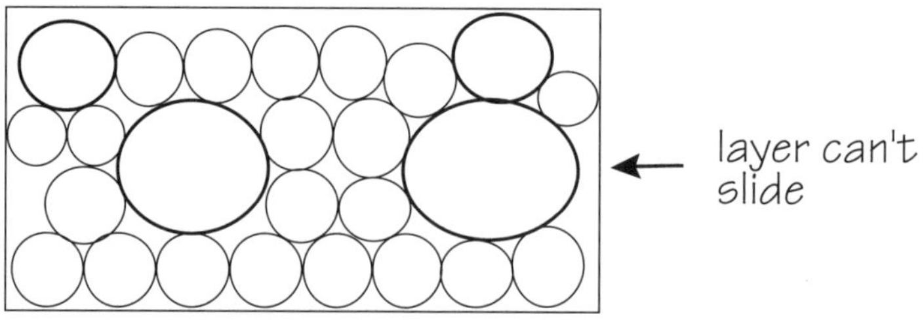

- e.g. (a) steel: iron, carbon, nickel, manganese, chromium.
  (b) dental filling: mercury, silver, iron.

Classifying materials

Questions

1 (**a**) Complete the table below

Particle	Mass Number	Number of Protons	Number of Neutrons	Number of Electrons	Electron Arrangement
Li atom		3	4		
Li^{+} ion					
^{13}C isotope	12			6	
^{12}C isotope	13	6			
Ne atom			10	10	
S^{2-} ion	32			18	

(**b**) Which of the above particles have the inert gas electron arrangement?

____

2 Draw an aluminium atom $^{27}_{13}Al$.

3 By means of a suitable diagram show the bonding between $^{24}_{12}Mg$ and $^{16}_{8}O$

4 All atoms of the same element contain the same number of __________ and __________.

5

	Melting point	Conducts when solid	Conducts when molten
A	high	yes	yes
B	low	no	no
C	high	no	yes

(**a**) Which could be aluminium? ____________________

(**b**) Which could be sodium chloride? ____________________

(**c**) Which could be water? ____________________

Patterns of behaviour

Periodic table

- **Periodic table** – elements arranged in **increasing atomic number.**

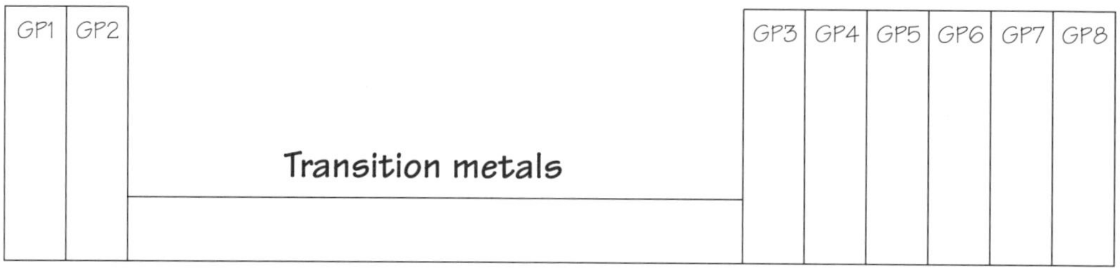

- Elements with **similar properties** are in **groups** (**columns**) – have **same** number of electrons in **outer shell.**
- Gradual change in property and reactivity **from top** of group **to bottom**.
- **Metals** more reactive **at bottom** of group.
- **Non-metals** more reactive at **top** of group.
- Metals in **groups 1, 2** and **3** – form **positive ions.**
- Non-metals in **groups 4, 5, 6, 7** – form **negative ions.**
- **Group 8** (O) – chemically **unreactive** – exist as **single atoms.**

Learn trends

Group 1 trends

less reactive metal

m.pt/b.pt **decreasing** ↓ Li, Na, K, Rb ↓ reactivity **increasing**

very reactive metal

Group 7 trends

very reactive gas

m.pt/b.pt **increasing** ↓ F, CL, Br, I ↓ reactivity **decreasing**

unreactive solid

Group 1 – alkali metals

Learn the reactions of **one** element in each group

- Metals **stored** under **oil** – very reactive.
- React violently **with water** making **hydrogen gas** and **alkaline solutions:**

$$2Li(s) + 2H_2O(l) \longrightarrow 2LiOH(aq) + H_2(g)$$

- Metals move on surface of water, cloudy solution – pH > 12.
- **React with non-metals** to form **ionic compounds** – metal carries a **+1 charge.**
- **Shiny** when cut but **tarnish** rapidly in air (oxygen):

i.e. $4Li(s) + O_2(g) \longrightarrow 2Li_2O(s)$

Properties and uses of alkali metal compounds

- **Are ionic** – high m.pt/b.pt, soluble in water, conduct in molten/aqueous form.
- **NaCl** – making chlorine, sodium hydroxide and hydrogen (electrolysis), gritting roads, diet.

Group 7 – Halogen

- **Non-metals** – exist as molecules with 2 atoms (**diatomic**) – Cl–Cl
- Have **coloured vapours** (F_2 – pale yellow, Cl_2 – green, Br_2 – red / orange, I_2 – purple) – colour darkens down the group.

- **Form ionic salts** with metals – halogen atom carries a **1- charge** (**halide ion**).
- **Corrosive** and toxic.

Similar property – same number of electrons in **outer shell** (energy level) – higher it is in the group the more easily it gains electrons:

- Fluorine readily gains electrons to give F^- – strong oxidising agent
- Iodine less readily gains electrons to give I^- – weak oxidising agent

Reactivity explained

Reactions of halogens

- **More** reactive element **displaces** less reactive ion from solution e.g. F_2 will **displace** Cl^- but Br_2 will **not displace** Cl^- ions:

$$F_{2(g)} + 2Cl^-_{(aq)} \rightarrow 2F^-_{(aq)} + Cl_{2(g)}$$
$$Cl_{2(g)} + 2Br^-_{(aq)} \rightarrow 2\,Cl^-_{(aq)} + Br_{2(l)}$$

Can put other elements into reactivity order by displacement

Uses of halogens

- Water purification, **making** bleaches, disinfectants, pesticides, antiseptics.

Uses of halogen compounds

- **Silver halides** – photography.
- **Fluorides** – tooth pastes and water supply.
- NaCl as above.

Properties and uses of group 8 (0) – noble gases

- Have full outer electron shells.
- Very **unreactive** gases – exist as **single atoms**.
- **Ar** – in filament bulbs.
- **Ne** – electrical discharge tubes (**sign making**).
- **He** – air ships (balloons).

Transistion metals

Between groups 2 and 3 – they have:

- **high** m.pt/b.pt, high densities and **very** hard – strong – used in construction, e.g. iron and alloys.
- form **coloured** compounds.
- act as **catalysts,** e.g.
  - **Ni** – making margarines
  - **Pt** – oxidation of ammonia to make nitric acid
  - **Fe** – Haber process – making ammonia
  - V_2O_5 – contact process – makes sulphuric acid
- **compounds** used in paints and dyes, breathalysers, cereals, medicines.

These are typical metals

Patterns of behaviour

Questions

1 Study the section of the periodic table below and answer the questions which follow.

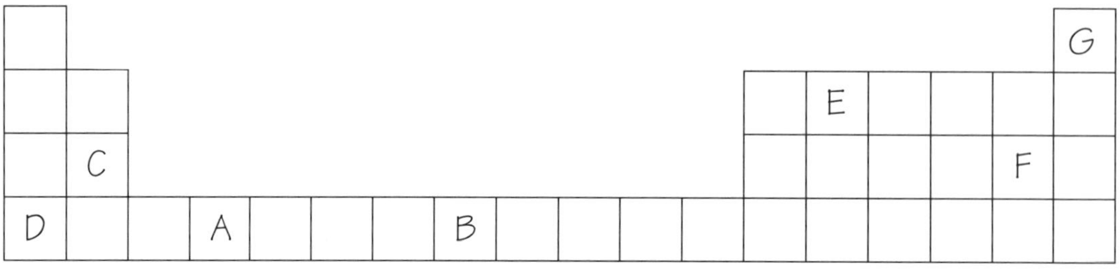

(**a**) Which of the above elements are metals? ________________

(**b**) Which element has atomic number 6? ________________

(**c**) Which element forms an oxide which dissolves in water and turns universal indicator solution violet? ________________

(**d**) Write a chemical equation for the reaction of Ca with oxygen. ________________

2 (**a**) The element sodium (Na) is found in group ______ called the_______ _______.
The metal is stored_______ _______because it_______violently with_______.

(**b**) A small piece of sodium is added to water. Describe what you will see happening.

____

____

3 The element Fe is used as a catalyst in the _______ process for making_______.

4 Ne and Ar are called_______ _______because they do not_______with anything else. They are found in group_______.

5 Bromine (Br) in group_______called the_______is less reactive than chlorine.

Chlorine gas was bubbled into an aqueous solution containing bromide ions.
Write an ionic equation for the reaction. ________________
This reaction is called a________________ ________________.

6 List 3 ways in which transition metals differ from group 1 metals.

____

____

7 From the list: bromine, chlorine, iodine, silver bromide and sodium chloride, give:
(**a**) halogen which is a liquid at room temperature. ________________
(**b**) chemical found in sea water but not in fresh water. ________________
(**c**) a substance broken down by light. ________________

Materials & their properties

Changing materials

This section provides notes on:

- **extraction – obtaining metals from their ores.**
- **synthesis – building new substances from elements or simpler compounds.**

Examples – extracting iron from iron ore, and aluminium from bauxite.
– synthesising ammonia (NH_3) from nitrogen and hydrogen.

- **Raw material** – substance which occurs **naturally** (**in nature**) – may *not* be starting materials for the chemical reaction.

Some important points about extracting metals from their ores:

- **ores** – are either metal oxides *or* substances which can be changed into metal oxides, usually by roasting.
- **reduction** – removal of oxygen from oxides leaving metal.

Always describe industrial processes

Reduction method depends upon position of metal in activity series.

- Metals **high** in series – e.g. sodium, calcium, aluminium – can only be reduced by **electrolysis.**
- Metals **low** in series – e.g. iron, copper – can be reduced using **carbon** *or* **carbon monoxide** *or* **by more reactive metal,** *e.g.* Zn.

Extracting iron from iron ore

Very common question

- **Iron ore** usually used is **haematite** – Fe_2O_3.
- **Raw materials** are **haematite** (Fe_2O_3), **coke** (C), limestone ($CaCO_3$).
- Limestone added to remove impurities such as sand (SiO_2).

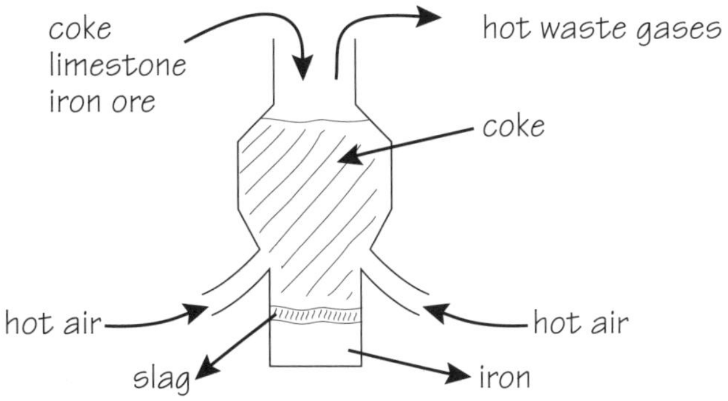

- Energy from hot gases removed to save energy/cost

The process

- Iron, coke and limestone are crushed, mixed and loaded into top of furnace.
- A blast of very hot air is blown into mixture to make reaction work.
- **Coke burns in hot air (oxygen) → carbon dioxide + heat.**
- **Carbon dioxide reacts with more coke → carbon monoxide.**
- **Carbon monoxide reduces (removes oxygen) from haematite → iron.**
- **Limestone reacts with sand and other impurities → slag.**
- **Molten iron sinks to bottom.**
- **Molten slag floats on the iron.**

Equations for the reaction

1 coke + oxygen → carbon dioxide + heat
$C(s) + O_2(g) \rightarrow CO_2(g)$

You must be able to write balanced equations

This reaction **gives out heat** – **exothermic.**

2 carbon dioxide + coke → carbon monoxide
$CO_2(g) + C(s) \rightarrow 2CO(g)$

3 carbon monoxide + haematite → iron + carbon dioxide
$3CO(g) + Fe_2O_3(s) \rightarrow 2Fe(l) + 3CO_2(g)$

4 limestone + sand → slag + carbon dioxide
$CaCO_3(s) + SiO_2(s) \rightarrow CaSiO_3(s) + CO_2(g)$

Reactive element will displace less reactive one

Making steel

- Iron from blast furnace is **brittle – called cast iron.**
- **Cast iron** is converted into steel by **removing excess carbon.**
- **Oxygen** is **blown through** cast **iron** to **burn carbon** away.
- Sometimes small amounts of other metals, e.g. nickel, manganese, chromium, added to produce an **alloy** (**mixture**) – **produce a special steel** such as **stainless steel.**

Uses of slag

- Insulation, road building, building materials

Electrolysis

- **Breaking down a substance containing ions,** e.g. molten compound or aqueous solution using electricity. Very expensive method.

Some important points about electrolysis

- Substance **must** be **molten** (**melted / fused**) state or **dissolved** in water.
- **Direct current** needed.
- Ions are **free to move about** in the molten or aqueous form.
- Electrodes – ions are discharged.
- **Not** AC – no ion movement.

Apparatus needed

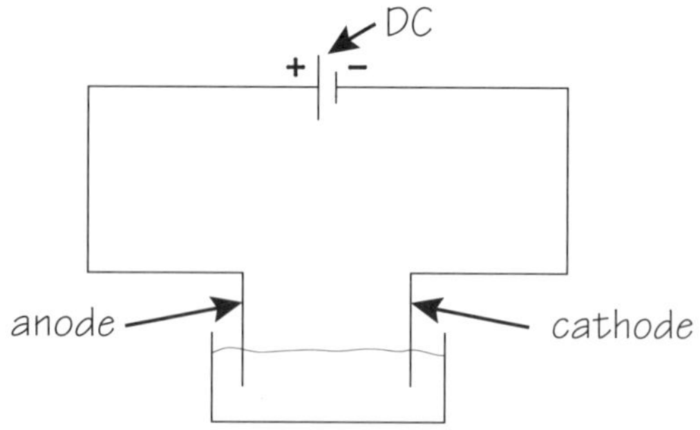

Common substances which can undergo electrolysis

- All acids / alkalis
- Ionic compounds, e.g. NaCl, Al_2O_3.
- ***Generally covalent compounds do not conduct.***

Comparison between electrolysis and conduction in a wire

Give clear unambiguous answers

Electrolysis	*Conduction (wire)*
ions carry the current	electrons carry the current
substance broken down	no change to wire
no current when no ions left	current passes indefinitely

Electrolysis – extracting reactive metals

- **groups 1, 2 and 3** of periodic table.
- **Molten/fused purified metal compounds used.**
- **Salts added** (e.g. cryolite) → **lower melting point** → **increase electrical conductivity** → **economical.**

Extracting aluminium from bauxite (Al_2O_3)

- Large quantity of electricity used.

Label diagrams

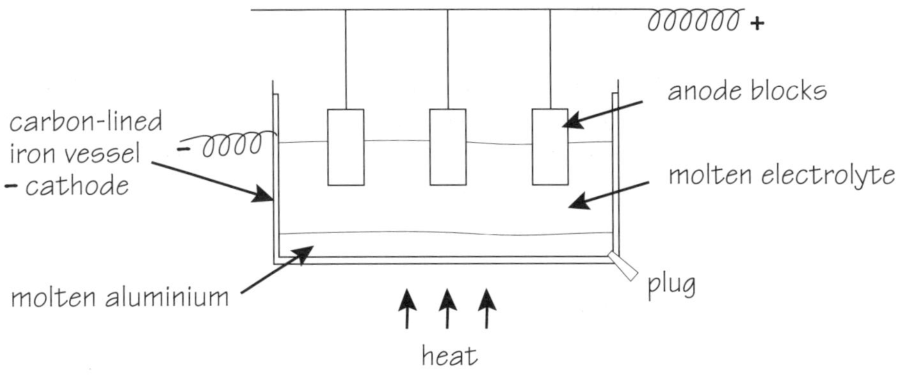

- Plants are built near power source and coast.
- **Raw materials** are **bauxite** and **cryolite.**
- Carbon (graphite) electrodes with **large surface area** → **speed up discharge.**
- They are **cheap** and **abundant.**

Ionic equations for the reactions:

1 **cathode:**

$Al^{3+}(l) + 3e^- \rightarrow Al(l)$

Al^{3+} **reduced** since it **gains electrons.**

Both versions ok

2 **anode:**

$2O^{2-}(l) - 4e^- \rightarrow 2O_2(g)$

or use

$2O^{2-}(l) \rightarrow 2O_2(g) + 4e^-$

O^{2-} **oxidised** since it **loses electrons.**

Carbon anodes react with **hot oxygen** – **erodes them** – **need replacing regularly** otherwise **discharge rate low.**

$C(s) + O_2(g) \rightarrow CO_2(g)$

- **Molten aluminium tapped off** → allowed to cool → useful materials made.
- Relate **main property** to its **application.**

Be precise with use and always give 2 unrelated uses

Uses of aluminium	**Property**
cooking utensils	good conductor of heat – doesn't corrode or melt
overhead electric cables	good electrical conductor – low density → light
window frames	strong and doesn't corrode
aeroplanes	strong and low density → light

Purification of metals by electrolysis

- Extractions not involving electrolysis form impure metals.
- 99+ % pure by electrolysis.

The process:

- impure metal makes anode.
- pure metal cathode – rotated.
- low DC current.
- electrolyte contains metal ions of impure metal.
- impurities drop to bottom of vessel.
- cathode increases in size.
- anode decreases in size.

Example: purification of copper metal

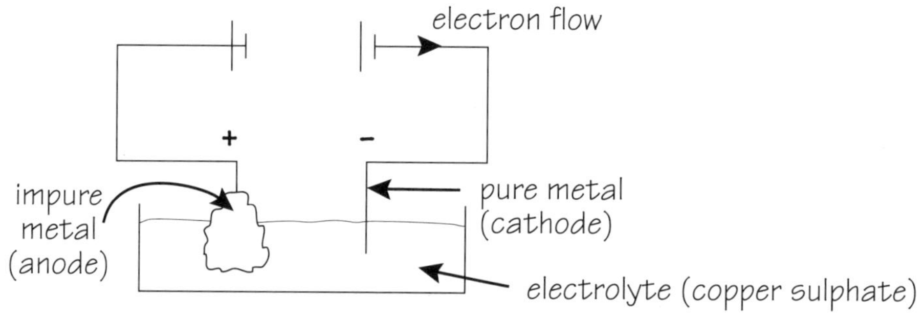

- **Same set-up for electroplating objects – object to be coated-cathode.**

Ionic equations for the reactions:

1 anode

$Cu(s) \rightarrow Cu^{2+}(aq) + 2e^-$

copper metal loses electrons → oxidised to **Cu^{2+} ions.**

2 cathode

$Cu^{2+}(aq) + 2e^- \rightarrow Cu(s)$

copper ion (**Cu^{2+}**) **gains electrons → reduced** to **Cu metal.**

As **RED**uction and **OX**idation happen together – **REDOX reactions.**

What you **see**, not what it is

The following **observations** are made when copper is purified:

- **blue electrolyte stays same colour intensity throughout.**
- **pink deposit on cathode → larger cathode.**
- **container heats up during electrolysis.**
- **anode gets smaller.**
- **impurities under anode.**

Useful products from air

Haber process – ammonia ($NH_{3(g)}$)

- Ammonia – raw material for making nitric acid, fertilisers, plastics etc.

Note difference between raw and starting materials

Starting materials:
- **nitrogen** (N_2) – fractional distillation of liquid air.
- **hydrogen** (H_2) from natural gas (CH_4) – reaction with steam at high temperature and pressure catalyst.

$$CH_4(g) + H_2O(g) \rightarrow CO(g) + 3H_2(g)$$

Raw materials are air and natural gas.
Equation for reaction:

$$N_2(g) + 3H_2(g) \rightleftharpoons 2NH_3(g) \quad \Delta H = -93 \text{ kJ/mole}$$

- Reaction is **reversible.**
- At equilibrium, speed of both reactions is **equal**.
- Occurs in closed container – (nothing leaves or enters the container).
- Industrial processes **do not** reach equilibrium (time consuming and costly).
- Concentration depends on reaction conditions.
- Le Chatelier's principle explains how conditions affect amounts of reactants and products.
  Conditions for **high yield** (amount) of **ammonia**:

Learn actual conditions

Predicted	Actual
high pressure	**high pressure** (200 atm)
low temperature	**moderately high temperature** (450°C)
remove ammonia	**remove ammonia**
catalyst	**catalyst** (**iron/iron oxide**)

The process
- Gases leaving – mixture of ammonia and **unchanged** nitrogen and hydrogen.
- Gases are **cooled** until ammonia (b.pt -33°C) condenses.
- **Unreacted** hydrogen and nitrogen **recycled**.

Le Chatelier's principle

Learn to apply this 'law'

– **whatever you do to the equilibrium, it does opposite**, e.g. **increase in temperature – equilibrium will try to decrease the temperature**.

Explanations for chosen conditions
We can make predictions using Le Chatelier's principle:
- ***endothermic reaction*** – temperature **increased** – yield of **product increases.**
- ***exothermic reaction*** e.g. (making ammonia) – temperature **increased** – yield of **product decreases.**

Examiners are keen on this

Understand the temperature anomaly:
- low temperature **should** give high yield.
- molecules have **lower energy** than **activation energy** barrier.
- so **collisions unsuccessful or very slow reaction** → **low yield.**

direction of equilibrium with decreased temperature →

$$N_2(g) + 3H_2(g) \rightleftharpoons 2NH_3(g) + \text{heat}$$

← *direction of equilibrium with increased temperature*

Pressure effect:
- pressure increase.
- number of particles (moles) decreases.
- equilibrium moves forming less particles.
- vice versa.

direction of equilibrium with increased pressure →

$$N_2(g) + 3H_2(g) \rightleftharpoons 2NH_3(g)$$

← *direction of equilibrium with decreased pressure*

- Yield higher for a higher pressure at fixed Temperature ($y_1 > y_2 > y_3$)

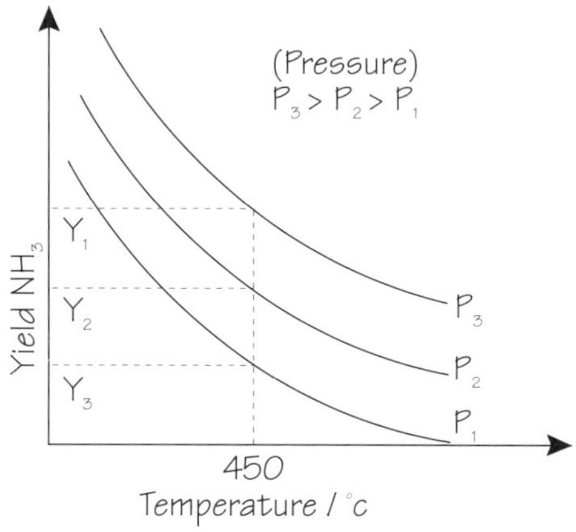

e.g. **for ammonia:** from equation
4 moles of gas on left makes **2 moles of gas** on right

Concentration effect:
- **increase** in reactant concentration ————> **increase** in products
- **removing** products ————> **decrease** in reactants
- factors are **optimised** in industrial process – so time and energy are **not wasted.**

e.g. **for ammonia:**
- temperature **raised** – allowing **successful collisions** – but **yield** goes **down.**
- **balance** – reasonable **rate** (**speed**) and adequate **yield** (see above conditions/**graph page 00**).
- ammonia yield – **11–14%.**
- **unreacted** nitrogen and hydrogen **recycled** – effective yield 100%.

N.B. 10°C increase in temperature = rate doubles

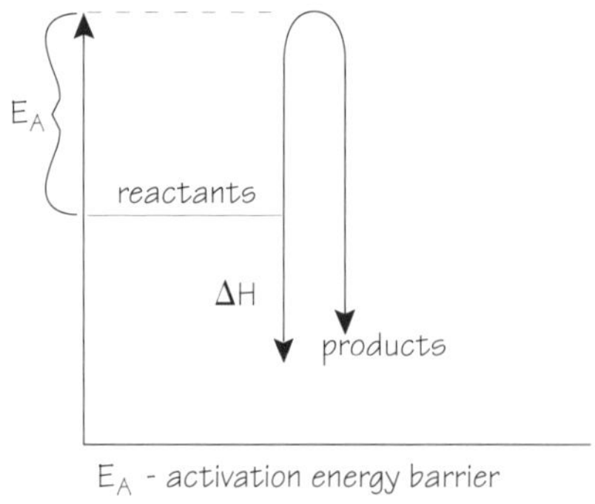

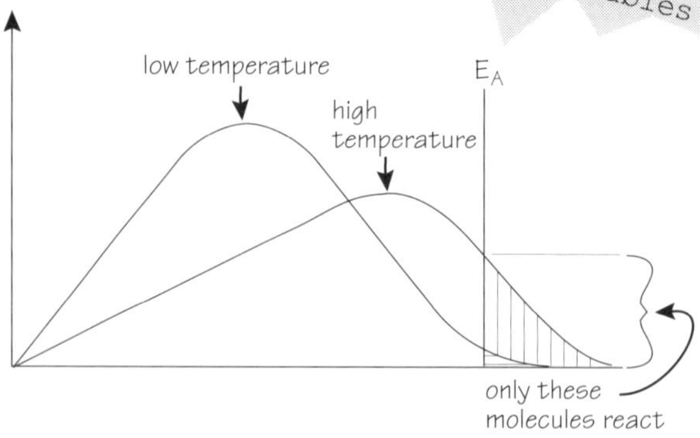

Fertilisers

Help to provide an adequate and rapid food supply:
- **increasing human population** → **needs more food** → **fertilisers provide essential elements,** e.g. N, for growing crops → **increased yields.**
- **plants cannot use nitrogen gas** → **soluble forms needed by roots** → nitrates or ammonium salts.

Learn this one

The process

- **ammonia oxidised** → **nitrogen oxides** NO_2 (s).
- **nitrogen oxides react with oxygen and water** → **nitric acid**.
- **nitric acid neutralises ammonia** *or* **ammonia solution** → **ammonium nitrate fertilisers.**
- **sulphuric / hydrochloric acid neutralises ammonia** *or* **ammonia solution** → **fertilisers**, *e.g.* ammonium sulphate and ammonium chloride.

Conversion of ammonia to nitric acid – equations for reactions:

1 ammonia + oxygen → nitrogen oxide + water (platinum catalyst at 900°C)
$4NH_3(g) + 5O_2(g) \rightarrow 4NO(g) + 6H_2O(g)$

2 nitrogen oxide + oxygen → nitrogen dioxide (brown gas)
$2NO(g) + O_2(g) \rightarrow 2NO_2(g)$

This reaction is **very fast.**

3 nitrogen dioxide + oxygen + water → nitric acid
$4NO_2(g) + O_2(g) + H_2O(l) \rightarrow 4HNO_3(l)$

- Nitric acid – typical strong acid – fully dissociated – pH <1.
- Ammonia dissolves in water to make **ammonia solution.**
  $NH_3(g) + H_2O(l) \rightleftharpoons NH^{4+}(aq) + OH^-(aq)$
- Contains ammonium ions (NH_4^+) and **hydroxide ions** (**OH^-**)
- **Partly dissociated** – a **weak** base (pH9 – only a **few OH^- ions** are formed).

Neutralisation of acids

Application of process important

Ionic equation for neutralisation process

$$H^+(aq) + OH^-(aq) \rightarrow H_2O(l)$$

- Strong acids are **fully dissociated** – **high H^+ ion** concentration – low pH.
- **with ammonia solution – forms nitrogenous fertilisers.**

Equations for the reactions:

acid + alkali → salt + water

e.g.

1 hydrochloric acid + ammonia solution → ammonium chloride + water
$HCl(aq) + NH_4OH(aq) \rightarrow NH_4Cl(aq) + H_2O(l)$

2 nitric acid + ammonia solution → ammonium nitrate + water
$HNO_3(aq) + NH_4OH(aq) \rightarrow NH_4NO_3(aq) + H_2O(l)$

Learn detailed method for preparation

3 sulphuric acid + ammonia solution → ammonium sulphate + water
$H_2SO_4(aq) + 2NH_4OH(aq) \rightarrow (NH_4)_2SO_4(aq)\ H_2O(l)$

Solid fertilisers made by **evaporation** of neutralised solution.

Higher percentage of nitrogen in fertiliser (see table) **the better as:**
- more effective for plant growth.
- less needed – easier storage and transportation.

Calculation – gain quick marks – always put down something

Fertiliser	Formula	Mass of one mole	Mass N in one mole	% of N
ammonium chloride	NH_4Cl	54.5 g	14 g	$\frac{14}{53} \times 100 = 27$
ammonium nitrate	NH_4NO_3	80 g	28 g	$\frac{28}{80} \times 100 = 35$
ammonium sulphate	$(NH_4)_2SO_4$	132 g	28 g	$\frac{28}{132} \times 100 = 21$

Problems with excessive use of fertiliser:
- May alter the pH of soil.
- Run off into rivers / lakes → **eutrophication.**
- Contamination of **drinking water** → **blue baby syndrome** and **cancer.**
- Harm animals and destroy **crumb** structure of soil.

Sulphuric acid: The contact process

raw materials: sulphur, air and **water**

Equilibrium reaction

The process

- **Sulphur is burnt in air → sulphur dioxide**
- **Sulphur dioxide reacts with more air → sulphur trioxide**
- **Sulphur trioxide reacts with concentrated sulphuric acid** (98%) → **oleum**
- **Oleum reacts with water → sulphuric acid**

Equations for the reactions:

1 Sulphur burns in air:

$$S_{(g)} + O_{2(g)} \rightarrow SO_{2(g)}$$

Can cause pollution → acid rain

2 sulphur dioxide + air + vanadium (V) oxide catalyst → sulphur trioxide

$$2SO_{2(g)} + O_{2(g)} \rightarrow 2SO_{3(g)} \ \Delta H = \text{exothermic}$$

1 atm makes 98%

equilibrium conditions: 450°C 1 atm (see Haber process page 49 for reasons)

3 sulphur trioxide + sulphuric acid → oleum

$$SO_{3(g)} + H_2SO_{4(l)} \rightarrow H_2S_2O_{7(l)}$$

Pressure increases yield but not worth it

4 oleum + → sulphuric acid

$$H_2S_2O_{7(l)} + H_2O_{(l)} \rightarrow 2H_2SO_{4(aq)}$$

NB sulphur trioxide not dissolved directly into water → fine mist

Reactions of dilute suphuric acid to makes salts

salts → hydrogen in acid replaced by a metal

Above hydrogen in series

Methods: reacts with

- reactive metals → salt + hydrogen
  $2Mg_{(s)} + H_2SO_{4(aq)} \rightarrow MgSO_{4(aq)} + H_{2(g)}$
- metal carbonates → salt + water + carbon dioxide
  $CuCO_{3(s)} + H_2SO_{4(aq)} \rightarrow CuSO_{4(aq)} + H_2O_{(l)} + CO_{2(g)}$
- metal oxides → salt = water
  $MgO_{(s)} + H_2SO_{4(aq)} \rightarrow MgSO_{4(aq)} + H_2O_{(l)}$
- alkali → salt + water (**neutralisation**)
  $2NaOH_{(aq)} + H_2SO_{4(aq)} \rightarrow Na_2SO_{4(aq)} + 2H_2O_{(l)}$
- hydrogencarbonates → salt + water + carbon dioxide
  $2NaHCO_{3(s)} + H_2SO_{4(aq)} \rightarrow Na_2SO_{4(aq)} + 2H_2O_{(l)} + 2CO_{2(g)}$

Same reactions with other acids

Ionic equation: $H_{(aq)}$ + **$OH_{(aq)}$** → **$H_2O_{(l)}$**

Use **titration** method → how much of the two solutions will just react → **indicator** → end point (phenolphthalein; pink in alkali → colourless in acid)

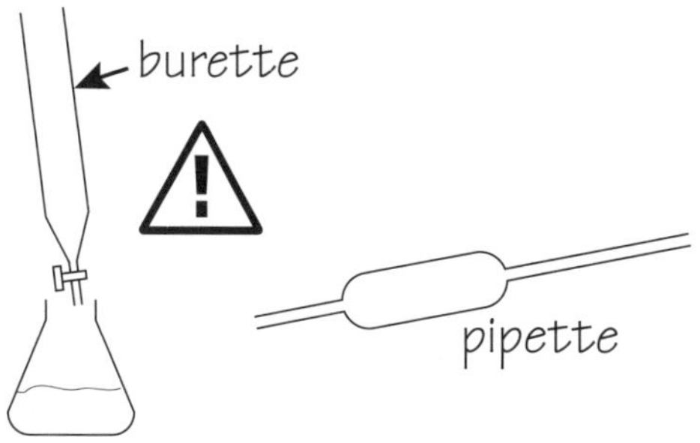

Example of calculation

25 cm^3 of 0.1 M HCl just react with 25 cm^3 NaOH. What is the concentration NaOH?

- Balanced equation for reaction: NaOH + HCl → NaCl + H_2O
  ratio 1 : 1
- 25 cm^3 0.1M HCl contains $\frac{25 \times 0.1}{1000} = 0.0025$ moles
- Moles of NaOH present in 25 cm^3 = 0.0025 as ratio 1:1
- Concentration of NaOH = $\frac{0.0025}{25} \times 1000 = 0.1$ M

Precipitation

Two soluble salts mixed → soluble salt + insoluble salt (precipitate)
e.g. sodium chloride + silver nitrate → sodium nitrate + silver chloride (insoluble)
$NaCl_{(aq)} + AgNO_{3\,(aq)} \rightarrow NaNO_{3(aq)} + AgCl_{(s)}$ (see halogen (group 7) page 42)

General rule

NB all group 1 salts and all nitrate compounds are soluble including lead, silver, and carbonate compounds → insoluble

Reaction of concentrated sulphuric acid

Dehydrating / drying agent → remove water / or elements of water from substance

1 **Drying agent:** to dry many gases – e.g. chlorine

- *Not* ammonia gas (alkaline) or ethene → react

use as test for water

2 Dehydrating agent:

e.g. hydrated blue copper (II) sulphate crystal → anhydrous white copper (II) sulphate crystals + water

$$CuSO_4.5H_2O_{(s)} \rightarrow CuSO_{4(s)} + 5H_2O_{(g)}$$

- **water of crystallisation is lost**

  sugar → carbon + water

  $C_6H_{12}O_{6(s)} \rightarrow 6C_{(s)} + 6H_2O_{(g)}$

- **hydrogen** and **oxygen removed from compound** → **water**

3 Oxidising agent → reduced to sulphur dioxide gas

copper + sulphuric acid → copper sulphate + sulphur dioxide + water

- $Cu_{(s)} + 2H_2SO_{4(l)} \rightarrow CuSO_{4(aq)} + SO_{2(g)} + 2H_2O_{(l)}$

  oxidised reduced

- carbon + sulphuric acid → carbon dioxide + sulphur dioxide + water

  $C_{(s)} + 2H_2SO_{4(l)} \rightarrow CO_{2(g)} + 2SO_{2(g)} + 2H_2O_{(l)}$

  oxidised reduced

Acids and alkali

substances which dissolve in water → solution → acid or alkaline or neutral

- pH – concentration of hydrogen ions (H^+) in solution

Acids

- High (H^+) → low pH → strong acid → fully ionised → only ions present

e.g. sulphuric, hydrochloric and nitric acid

$$HCl(g) + H_2O_{(l)} \rightarrow H^+(aq) + Cl^-(aq)$$

pH = 1 or 2

- Low (H^+) → high pH → weak acid → partially ionised → few ions formed → equilibrium

e.g. methanoic and ethanioc acid

$$CH_3COOH_{(l)} + H_2O_{(l)} \rightleftharpoons H^+(aq) + CH_3COO^-(aq)$$

pH = 3 or 4

ionisation determines strength

NB **0.1 M HCl acid and 0.1 M ethanoic acid** → both **same concentration** → same number of particles

But **HCl is stronger** acid than ethanoic acid → **fully ionised – ethanoic is partially ionised**

Alkalis

- Strong alkali → pH > 12 → fully ionised → hydroxide ions(OH^-) formed

e.g. sodium hydroxide

$$NaOH(s) + H_2O(l) \rightarrow Na^+(aq) + OH^-(aq)$$

- Weak alkali → pH < 12 → partially ionised → few hydroxide ions formed

e.g. ammonia solution pH = 9

$$NH_3(g) + H_2O(l) \rightleftharpoons NH_4^+(aq) + OH^-(aq)$$

Indicators

Colour change of indicator shows type of solution made.

Indicator	**Colour** acid	alkali	neutral
universal	red	blue	green
blue litmus	red	blue	blue (no change)
red litmus	red	blue	red (no change)
phenolpthalein	colourless	pink	colourless

Strength of solution measured on pH scale:

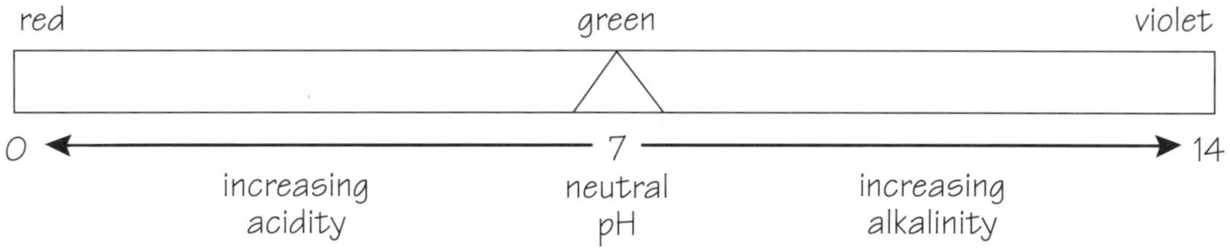

- acids pH < 7
- alkali pH >7
- **low** pH → **strong** acid
- **high** pH → **strong** alkali

Rusting

Rust – hydrated iron (III) oxide (Fe_2O_3) – reddy/brown
Metals react with air – **corrosion**
Iron corrodes → rusting – weakens metal – expensive to repair
Rusting speeded up by:

- oxygen
- water
- acids
- salty water / high temperatures

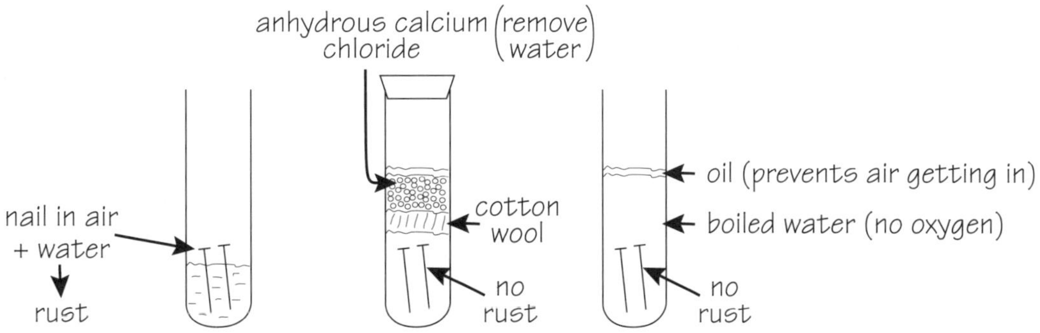

Prevention

Coating with paint, grease / oil, chrome plating – **barrier methods** – stops oxygen / water getting to metal.

- Sacrificial metals – galvanising (zinc) or another more reactive metal.

Iron reacts with dilute sulphuric acid in absence of oxygen → iron (II) sulphate + hydrogen

$$Fe_{(s)} + H_2SO_4(aq) \rightarrow FeSO_4(aq) + H_2(g)$$

In presence of oxygen (air) or concentrated sulphuric acid → iron (III) sulphate
Concentrated nitric acid makes iron 'passive' → unreactive

Alcohols

Contain an **OH group** in the molecule
Chemical family – homologous series – each substance differs from the next by a CH_2 unit – all react in similar way

General formula: $C_nH_{2n+1}OH$
e.g. $n = 1$ CH_3OH methanol, $n = 2$ C_2H_5OH ethanol

Structure

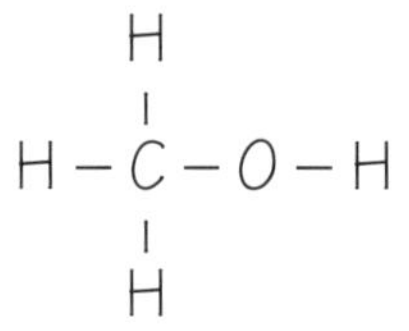

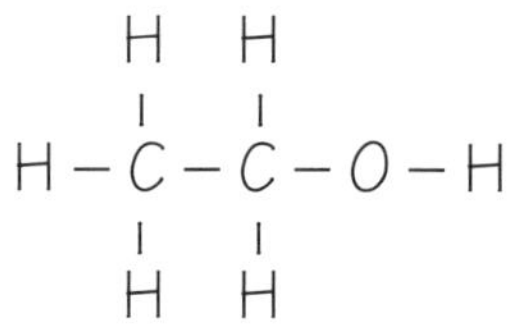

Preparation

1 By **fermentation** – to make beers, wines and spirits – action of yeast on glucose solution at 33°C (Anaeorbic respiration)

$$\underset{\text{glucose}}{C_6H_{12}O_6(aq)} \xrightarrow{\text{yeast}} \underset{\text{ethanol}}{2C_2H_5OH(aq)} + \underset{\text{carbon dioxide}}{2CO_2(g)}$$

2 Passing steam and ethene under pressure over a catalyst

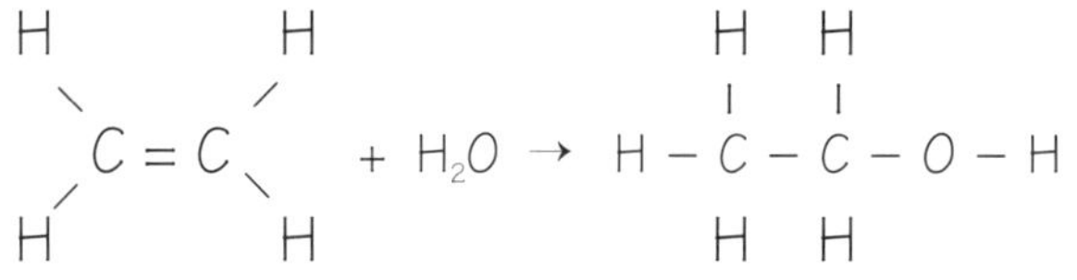

Properties of alcohols

Good fuel

Colourless liquids which mix with water

1 **Burn in air** → carbon dioxide and water

$2CH_3OH_{(l)} + 3O_{2(g)} \rightarrow 2CO_{2(g)} + 4H_2O_{(g)}$ ΔH = negative

2 **React with sodium metal** → salt and hydrogen

$2C_2H_5OH_{(l)} + 2Na_{(s)} \rightarrow 2C_2H_5O^- Na^+_{(g)} + H_{2(g)}$

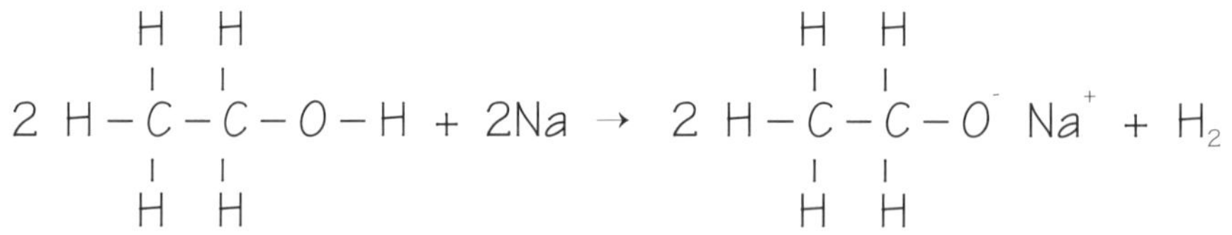

(cf. reaction water + sodium → 'salt' + hydrogen)
($2H_2O_{(l)} + 2Na_{(s)} \rightarrow 2NaOH_{(aq)} + H_{2(g)}$)

3 React with organic acids $\xrightarrow{\text{conc. } H_2SO_4 \text{ catalyst}}$ esters = water (reversible reaction)

$CH_3OH_{(l)}$ methanol + $CH_3COOH_{(l)}$ ethanoic acid $\xrightleftharpoons{H^+}$ $CH_3COOCH_{3(l)}$ methylethanoate + $H_2O_{(l)}$ water

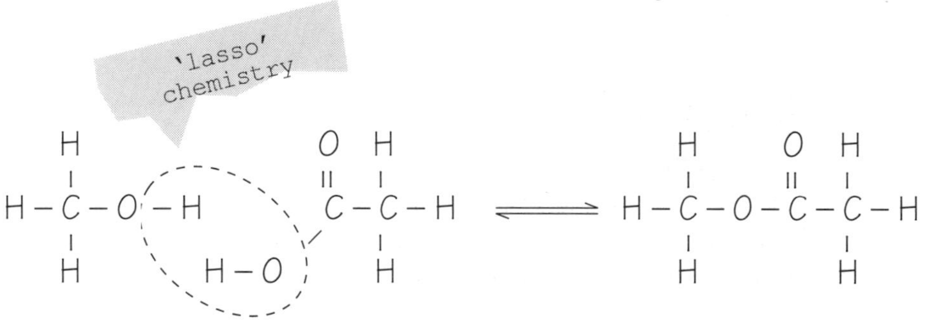

sweet fruity smell – flavouring in food

4 Oxidised by air / acidified potassium permanagate solution [O] → carboxylic acids (organic acids)

$C_2H_5OH_{(1)} + 2[O] \rightarrow CH_3COOH_{(1)} + H_2O_{(2)}$

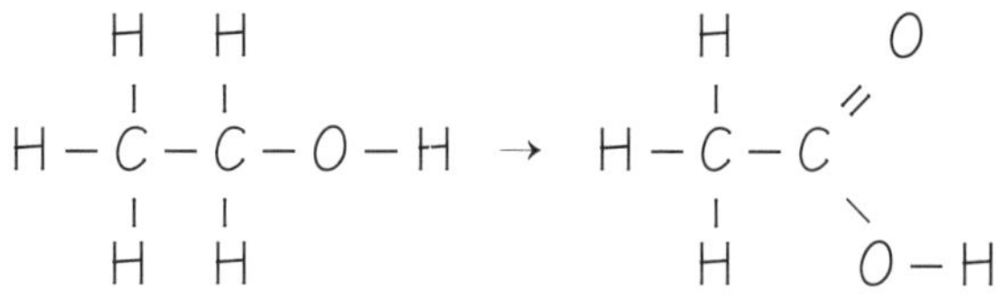

e.g. air → wine → ethanoic acid (taste sour)

Carboxylic acids (**organic acids**) – **contain COOH group** – **partly ionised** in **solution** – **weak acids** – **pH 3**

Reactions similar to hydrochloric acid / sulphuric acid.

methanoic acid ethanoic acid

Preparation

-oate = from acid
-yl = from alcohol

Oxidation of alcohols
e.g. ethanol + 2[O] → ethanoic acid + water

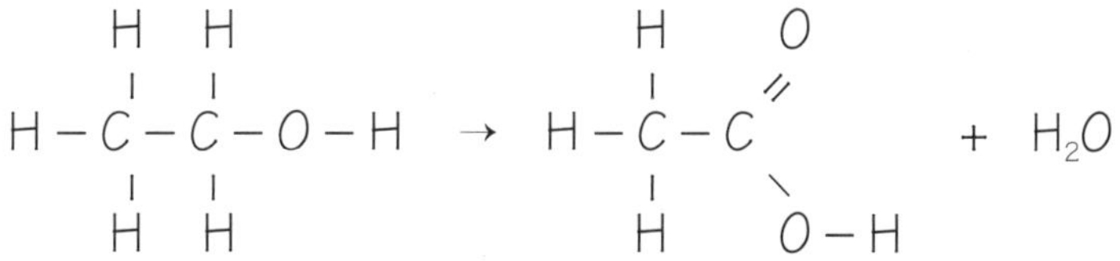

React with

N.B. similarities with HCl, H_2SO_4

1 Alkali → salt + water
methanoic acid + sodium hydroxide → sodium methanoate + water

ethanoic acid + sodium hydroxide → sodium ethanoate + water

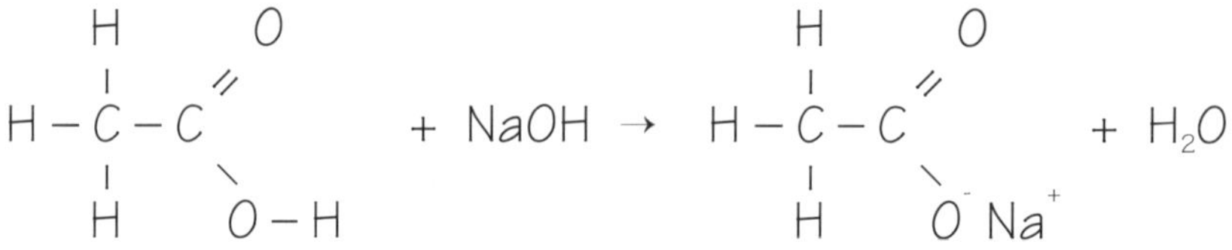

2 Alcohols → esters (see alcohols)

Solubility

Number of grams of substance → dissolved in 100 grams of water (solvent) → saturated solution → at given temperature

Solubility of solids increases with temperature
- **Solubility of all gases decreases with temperature**
- **Increased pressure → solubility of gas increases** (e.g. fizzy drinks)

Measuring solubility at different temperature – **solubility curves – comparisons of solubility**
e.g.

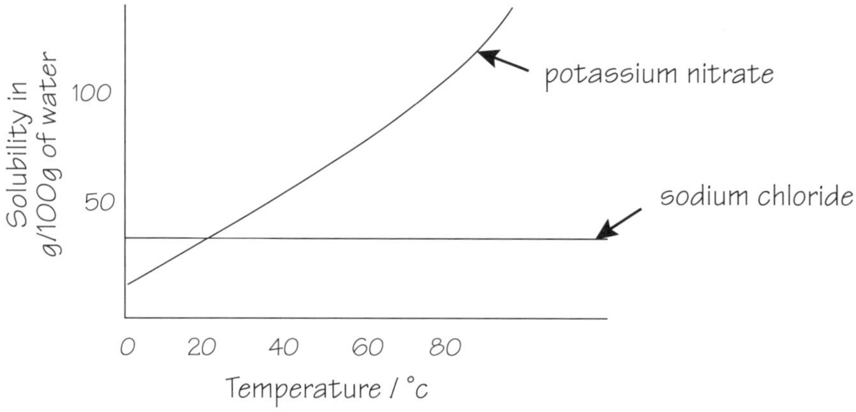

From graph
- Potassium nitrate **more soluble** than sodium chloride at **all temperatures** > 20°C
- Solubility of potassium nitrate in **hot** water **greater** than **cold**
- Solubility of sodium chloride **hardly changes**

Cooling a saturated solution → less solid dissolves → crystallisation occurs → solid forms → settles
e.g.

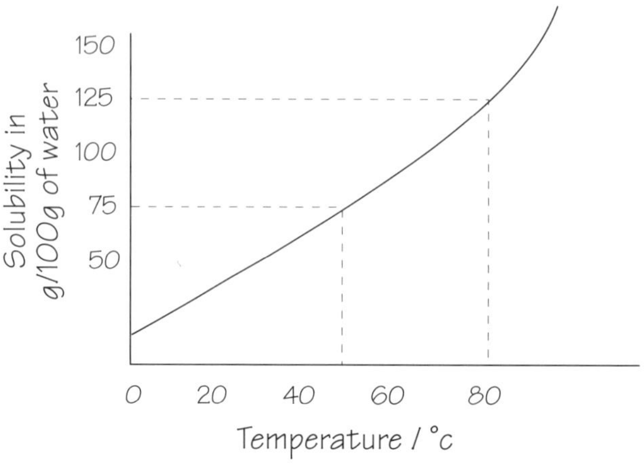

Solution cooled from 80°C to 50°C 125 - 75 g of crystals form i.e. 50 g

Water

Good **solvent** – dissolves compounds (**solute**) → **solution**

Hard and soft water

Water from different rocks → dissolves minerals → hard or soft water

- **Hard water – dissolved calcium and magnesium compounds** – high concentrations → very hard water
- **Soft water – little or no dissolved calcium or magnesium compounds**

Two types of hardness:

1 **Permanent** – removed by:

- **distillation** → very pure water – expensive
- **washing soda (sodium carbonate)** → insoluble calcium carbonate → precipitates → calcium / magnesium salts removed → soft impure water – soap lathers easily

$$Na_2CO_{3(s)} + CaSO_{4(aq)} \rightarrow CaCO_{3(s)} + Na_2SO_{4(aq)}$$

washing soda, hardness, calcium carbonate

- ion exchange resin → removes **calcium / magnesium ions** → replaces with **hydrogen** or **sodium ions** → soft impure water – soap lathers easily

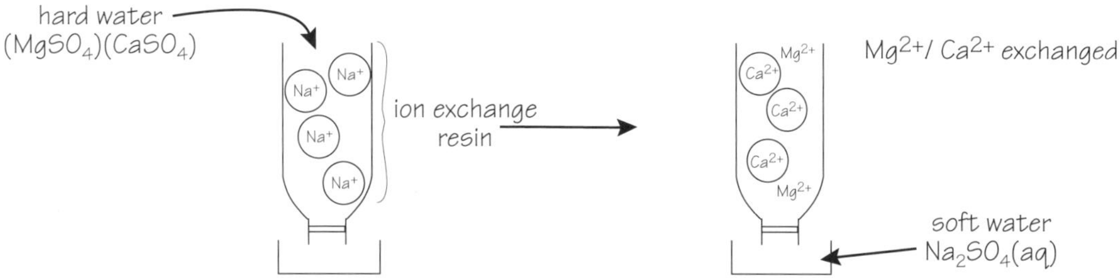

2 Temporary hardness

Carbon dioxide → rain → calcium carbonate rock → calcium hydrogen carbonate → hard water → boiling → decomposes calcium hydrogen carbonate → soft water and 'fur'

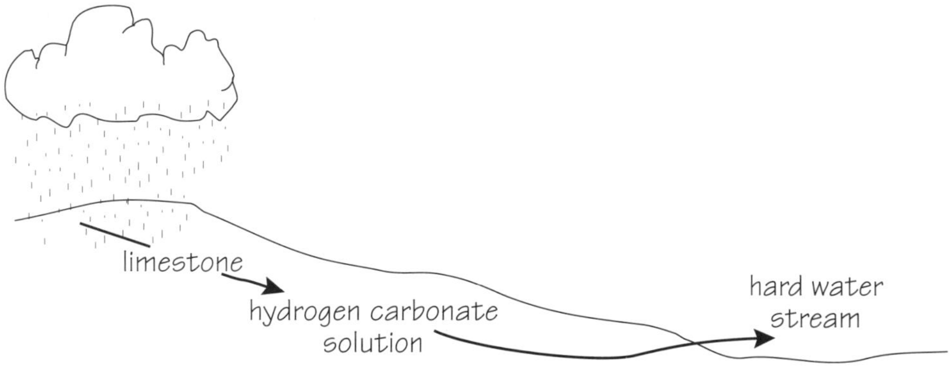

i.e.

$$\underbrace{CO_{2(g)} + H_2O_{(l)}}_{\text{rain water}} + \underset{\text{rock}}{CaCO_{3(s)}} \rightarrow \underset{\text{calcium hydrogen carbonate(aq)}}{Ca(HCO_3)_{2(aq)}}$$

$$Ca(HCO_3)_{2(aq)} \xrightarrow{heat} CaCO_{3(s)} + CO_{2(g)} + H_2O_{(l)}$$

temporary hardness (calcium hydrogencarbonate) → 'fur' precipitated (calcium carbonate)

detergents do not form scum they lather immediately

Disadvantages of hard water

- Water + soap → scum

e.g.

calcium sulphate + sodium stearate → calcium stearate + sodium sulphate
(hardness) (soap) (**scum**)

Soaps clean effectively when all hardness has gone

- Furs up kettles, boilers and pipes → dangerous
- Uses up more electricity to heat water

Size of hole gets smaller

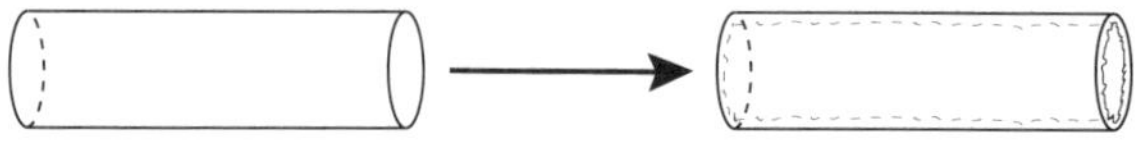

Advantages of hard water

Good health → strong teeth and bones, prevents heart disease

Water purification

Water in streams / rivers → reservoir → sand beds → filtered → remove mud / most bacteria → chlorinated → kills all bacteria → safe drinking water → homes

Water cycle

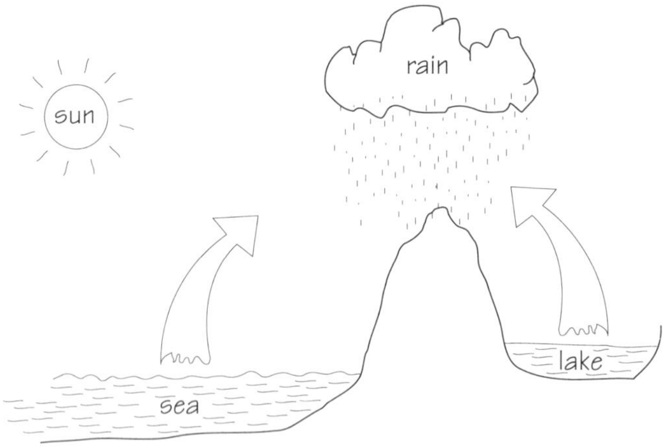

Water for homes

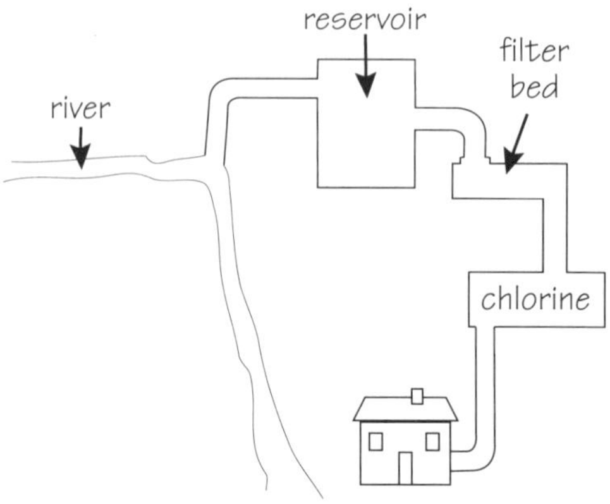

Chemical equations

Represent chemical reactions.

Can be shown as:

- **word equations** – reaction is written in words.
- balanced equations – reaction is written using formulae.
- ionic equations – only ions taking part are shown.

You must be able to write all types of equations

e.g. word equation methane + oxygen → carbon dioxide + water

balanced equation $CH_{4(g)} + 2O_{2(g)} \rightarrow CO_{2(g)} + 2H_2O_{(g)}$

ionic equation $2Cl^- \rightarrow Cl_2 + 2e^-$

$Fe^{3+} + 3e^- \rightarrow Fe$

Calculations using formula and equations

We can use formula and equations to calculate how much of a substance is used or how much is formed in a chemical reaction. For this we use the **mole**.

Never learn numbers for calculation

- **Solids** – 1 mole – atomic or molecular mass in grams.
  e.g. sodium chloride – NaCl: Na = 23, Cl = 35.5, NaCl = 23 + 35.5 = 58.5, 1 mole of NaCl = 58.5g.
- **Solutions** – when 1 mole of substance is dissolved and solution made up to $1dm^3$ – resulting solution is a **molar solution**.
  e.g. molar hydrochloric acid – M HCl contains 1 mole of HCl per dm^3 of solution. A solution containing 0.1M HCl, contains 0.1 moles of HCl per dm^3.
  The number of moles in a solution = $\frac{\text{mass in grams} \times \text{volume}}{\text{molecular mass} \times 1000}$ or $\frac{\text{molarity} \times \text{volume}}{1000}$
- ***Gases*** – number of moles of gas at room temperature = $\frac{\text{volume of gas } (cm^3)}{24\,000}$

Write a formula – gain a mark

Example of calculation

In the reaction $CH_{4(g)} + 2O_{2(g)} \rightarrow CO_{2(g)} + 2H_2O_{(g)}$
calculate the mass of carbon dioxide produced from 4g of methane.

(RAM C = 12, H = 1, O = 16)

- Calculate the molecular masses – CH_4 = 12 + 4 x 1 = 16, CO_2 = 12+ 2 x 16 = 44
- From the equation: 1 mole of methane (CH_4) produces 1 mole of carbon dioxide (CO_2).
- So 16 g of methane produces 44 g of carbon dioxide.
- Therefore 4 g of methane produces 11 g of carbon dioxide.

Finding a formula from given information

Follow these simple steps:
e.g. gas contains 27.3 g of carbon and 72.7 g of oxygen. Find its formula.

Show all stages of calculations

	C	O
Mass or percentage	27.3g	72.7g
Divide by atomic mass	$\frac{27.3}{12}$	$\frac{72.7}{16}$
	= 2.28	= 4.54
Divide by lowest number (to find ratio of atoms)	$\frac{2.28}{2.28}$	$\frac{4.54}{2.28}$
Empirical formula = CO_2	= 1	= 2

Simplest ratio of atoms

Finding the mass from given information

Follow these simple steps:

e.g. aluminium oxide is electrolysed for 24 hours using a steady current of 3000A. Find amounts of aluminium and oxygen formed (Al = 27g and 96 000C needed to deposit ion with charge 1+).

- Balanced equation at cathode
  $Al^{3+} + 3e^- \longrightarrow Al$
- Charge passed $Q = I \times t$ (I current in amps and t time in **seconds**)
  $= 3000 \times 24 \times 60 \times 60 = 2.6 \times 10^8 C$
- From equation: 3 moles of electrons makes 1 mole Al (27 g)
  number of conlombs needed to deposit 1 mole Al = 3 x 96000 (charge of 3+)
- Therefore

$$\text{mole Al formed} = \frac{3000 \times 24 \times 60 \times 60}{3 \times 96\,000}$$

- Mass of aluminium = moles Al x 27 g (900 g).

Rules of reactions

Reaction can be **speeded** up by using a **catalyst** or **increasing** the following:

- concentration of reactant.
- surface area of a solid (smaller particles).
- temperature.
- pressure (only gaseous reactions).

Particles must have enough energy to **collide successfully** – **number and frequency** of collisions needs to be **high** for fast reaction.

Never put down catalyst unless you know it works for that reaction

Catalysts:

- **Alter** rate of reaction and specific for a **given** reaction
  e.g. MnO_2, V_2O_5, Pt and Fe or Fe_2O_3 (see periodic trends).
- Decrease activation energy barrier – allowing **more particles** with **lower energy** to react – reduces time and energy, therefore cost of reaction.

Enzymes

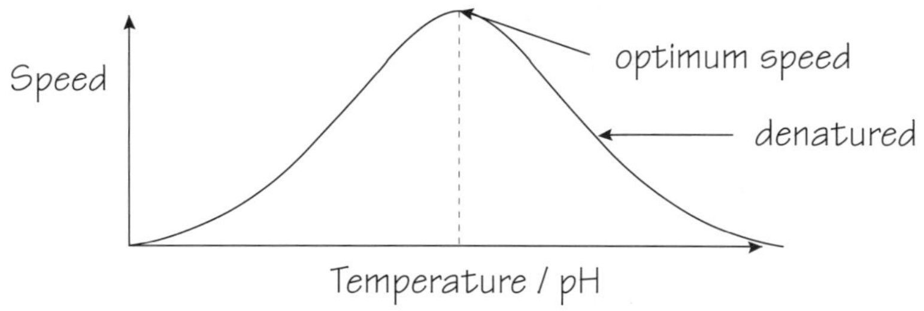

- Biological catalysts – **proteins** –
- structures **denatured** (damaged) above 45°C –
- **Specific** –
- Most effective at **optimum** conditions.

- **Low** temperature **decreases** enzyme and bacterial **activity** – helps to preserve food.

enzymes used for:
- baking (yeast) – makes **carbon dioxide** – bread rises.
- wine / beers (sugar / yeast) – makes alcohol (ethanol) – **anaerobic** (**fermentation**).
- dairy industry – cheese, yoghurts (**bacteria cultures**).

Reversible reactions

See details on ammonia manufacture. (page 49)

Reactant products are **constantly interchanged** but **concentrations** appear to be **constant.**

$$A + B \xrightleftharpoons{\text{reversible}} C + D$$

- Occur in a **closed** container.
- At equilibrium – speed of both forward and backwards reactions are **equal.**
- Reaction **conditions** determine concentrations (**Le Chatelier's principle**).

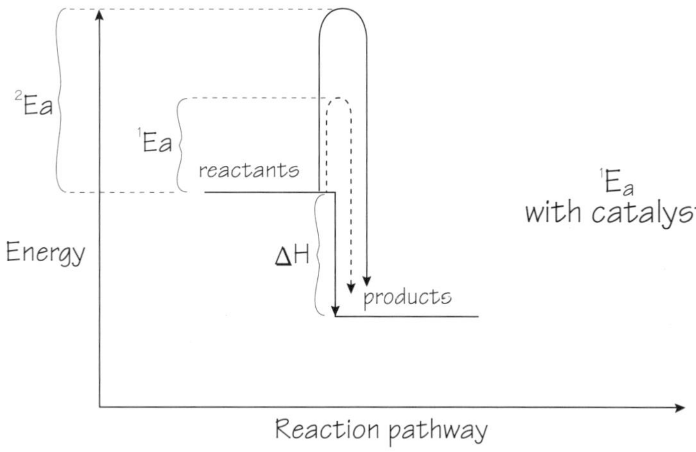

^1E_a with catalyst < ^2E_a without catalyst

ΔH **will not** alter with catalyst – **only** the **rate** of reaction will alter.

Rate graphs

Start of **flat** part of graph – reaction complete

Comparing reaction conditions on a graph

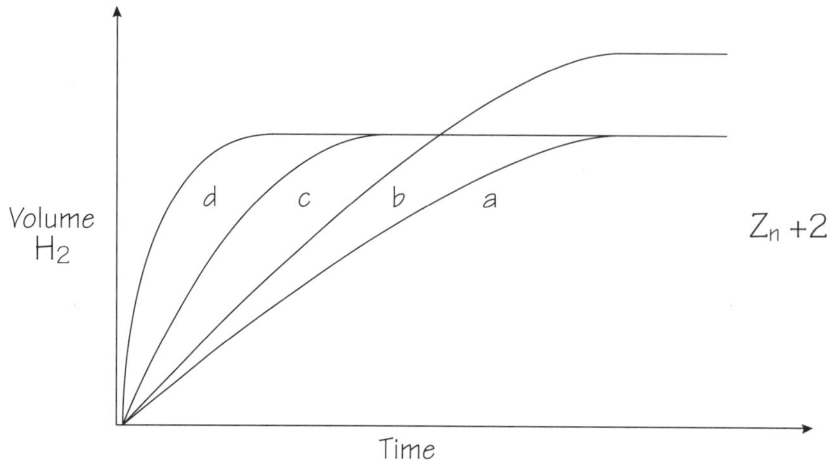

$Z_n + 2HCl \rightarrow Z_nCl_2 + H_2$

- c – reference graph (2 g Zn with excess acid).
- d – same amounts – powdered zinc / catalyst added ($CuSO_4$) or high temperature.
- a – large piece of zinc / weaker acid.
- b – more zinc used with excess acid.

Energy changes in chemical reactions

- **Exothermic** reactions – energy **given out** – temperature **rise** – ΔH = **negative**.
- **Endothermic** reactions – energy **taken in** – temperature **drop** – ΔH = **positive**.

Energy diagram

You must be able to draw energy diagrams

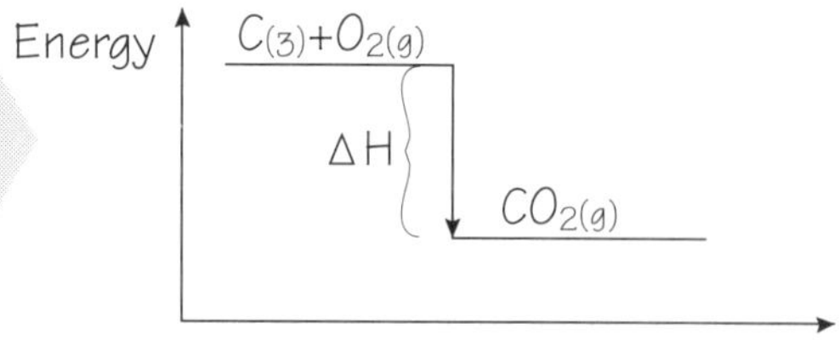

e.g. **All** burning fuels

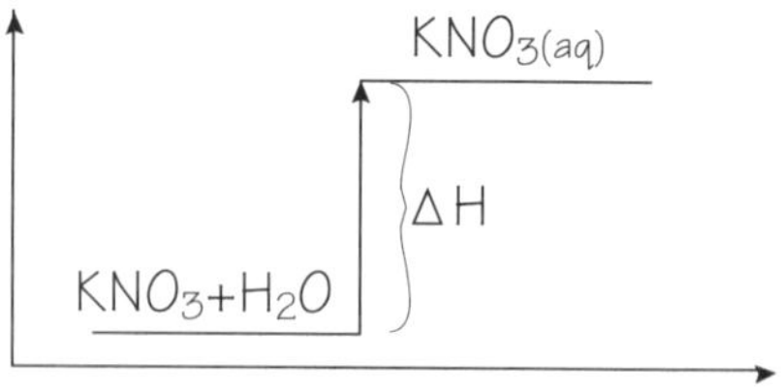

Potassium nitrate (aq)

NB Most reactions are exothermic.

During a chemical reaction

- Energy must be supplied to break bonds.
- Energy is released when bonds form.

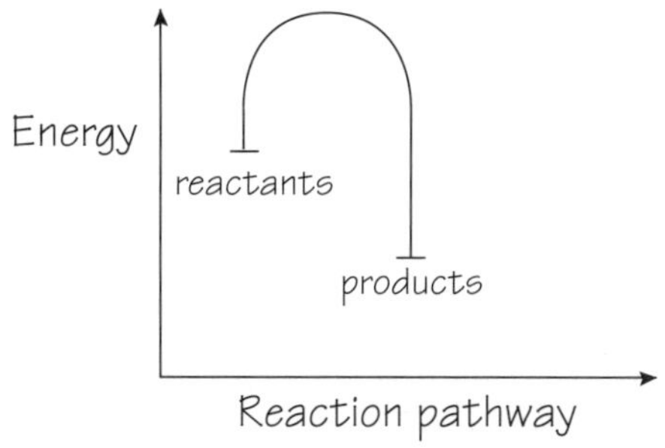

Exothermic

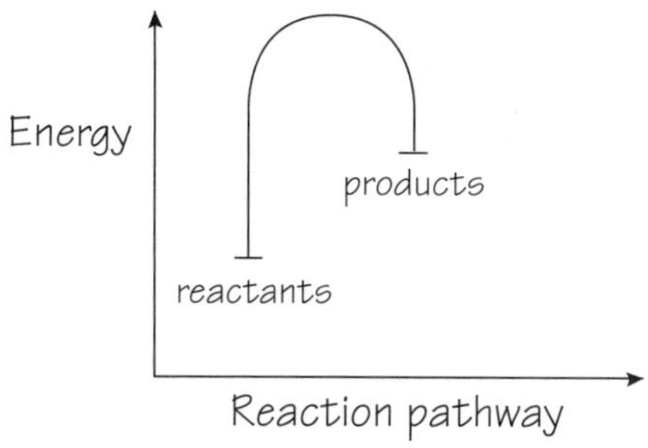

Endothermic

Calculating energy changes

Can use formulae and equations to calculate how much energy is used and how much is formed in a chemical reaction.
For this we use **bond energies**.

You may not need to break every bond in reactions

Example of a calculation

$CH_4 + 2O_2 \rightarrow CO_2 + 2H_2O$

- Calculate the energy change – is reaction endo / exothermic?
  bond energy: C-H = 413, O=O = 498 C=O = 803, O-H = 463 kJ/mol
- Calculate total energy to break the bonds (**+**):
  4 C-H bonds = 4 X 413 = 1652
  2 O=O bonds = 2 X 498 = 996
  Total = 2648 kJ
- Calculate the total energy when bonds are formed (-):
  2 C=O bonds = 2 x 803 = 1606
  4 O-H bonds = 4 x 463 = 1852
  Total 3458 kJ
- **Net change** = + 2648 - 3458 = - 810 kJ
- Reaction is **exothermic** – heat absorbed when bonds of CH_4 and O_2 broken **less than heat given out** when bonds CO_2 and H_2O formed.

Don't forget the **sign** (+ or -) and **units**.

Relate 810 kJ to exothermil energy diagram

Geological changes

- **Sedimentary rocks** – deposition of sediments in **layers** followed by compression by pressure – e.g. chalk, limestone, sandstone – **fossils between layers**.
- **Igneous rocks** – cooling down of **magma** (molten rock).
  – slow cooling – **intrusive** – granite (large crystals).
  – rapid cooling – **extrusive** – basalt (small crystals).
- **Metamorphic rocks** – action of **heat** and **pressure** on existing rock, e.g. limestone to **marble** and mudstone to **slate** – **interlocking crystals**.
- **Age of rocks** – by measuring radioactivity of rock sample.
- **S and P shock waves allow structure of earth to be worked out.**
  – **fast P waves travel through liquids and solids** –
  slow S waves travel only in solids.

Size of earthquake measured on the Reichter scale

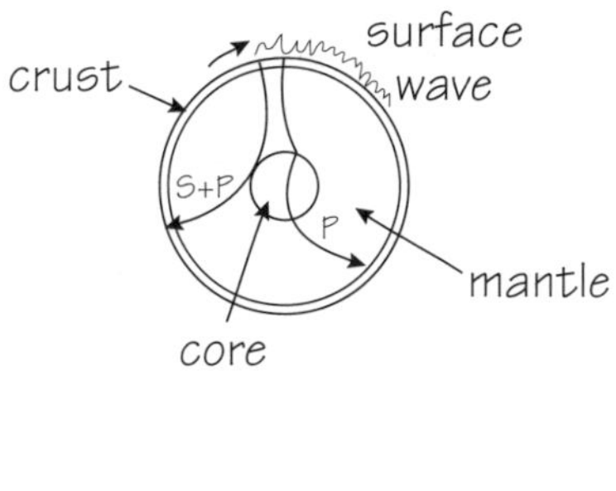

Seismograph trace

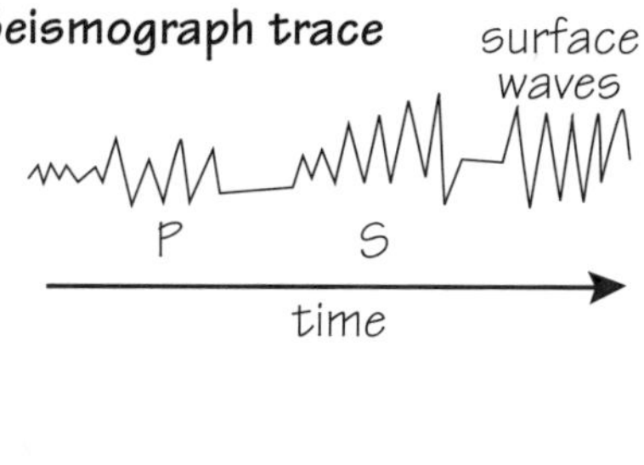

Plate tectonics

- Crust made of **number of plates**.
- **Radioactive processes** → **heat** → **convection currents within mantle** → **plates move** → result in **formation**, **deformation** and **recycling** of rock.
- Plates **sliding** past each other → earthquakes (e.g. San Andreas fault).
- Plates **move apart** – oceanic crust (mid-Atlantic ridge) → magma fills gap → basaltic oceanic rock – called **sea floor spreading** → magnetic stripes.
- Plates **collide** – thin dense oceanic crust **subducted** (**pushed down**) by thicker granitic continental plate → melts → earthquakes/volcanoes (e.g. Andes).

Diagram of rock cycle usually given – learn labels

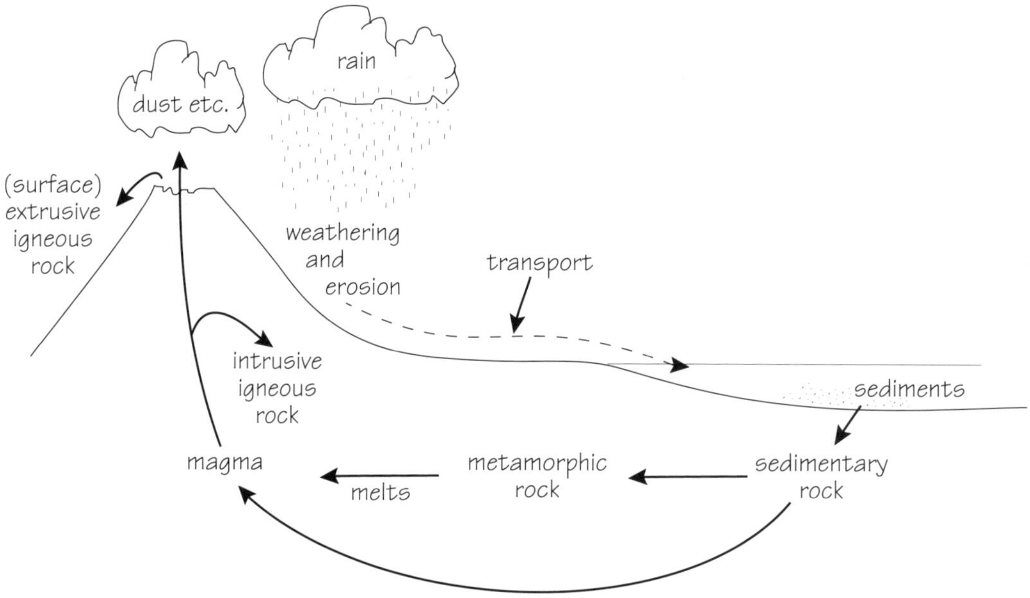

You must be able to explain *how* it happens

- **Weathering** and **erosion** also responsible for **recycling** of surface rock.
- Weathering – **breakdown** of rock by water, wind, animals, plant roots, chemicals.
- Erosion – **carrying away** of rock by water, wind, gravity.

Changes to the atmosphere

Volcanic activity released gases – formed original atmosphere – water vapour made oceans.

- **Initially** atmosphere CO_2, H_2O, methane and ammonia.
- Plants **changed** CO_2 to O_2 – into atmosphere – oxygen for breathing – carbon **locked** in plants formed **fossil fuels**.
- Methane and ammonia **reacted with oxygen** to form **nitrogen**.
- **Living organisms** and **denitrifying** bacteria made more **nitrogen**.
- Oxygen resulted in **ozone layer** – filtered **harmful** UV rays allowed **evolution**.
- Composition of atmosphere now **constant** – 79% N_2, 20% O_2, 1% noble gases, CO_2 and water.
- Kept constant by animals, plants and microorganisms (**carbon cycle**).

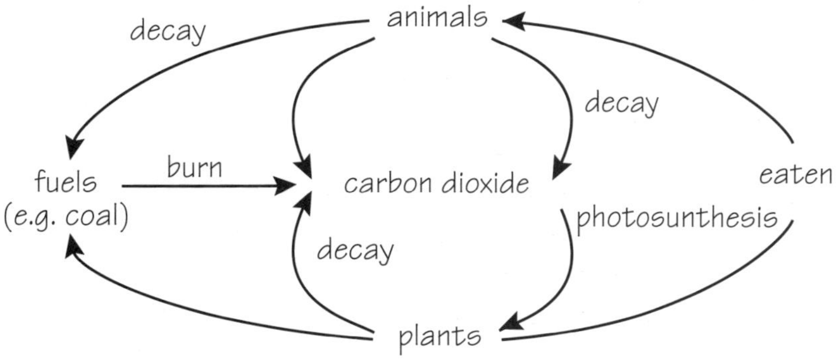

- **Burning fossil fuels – releases CO_2 in atmosphere → increase in CO_2 in atmosphere → reaction with sea water increases → making carbonate sediments → absorbs excess CO_2 → constant composition in atmosphere.**

Crude oil (petroleum) & hydrocarbons

- Crude oil (petroleum – formed in several steps over **millions of years**: sea creatures die → sink to sea bed → covered by rock → heat and pressure causes them to decay → oil and gas.
- Crude oil can be separated into **fractions** according to their **boiling points** by **fractional distillation**.

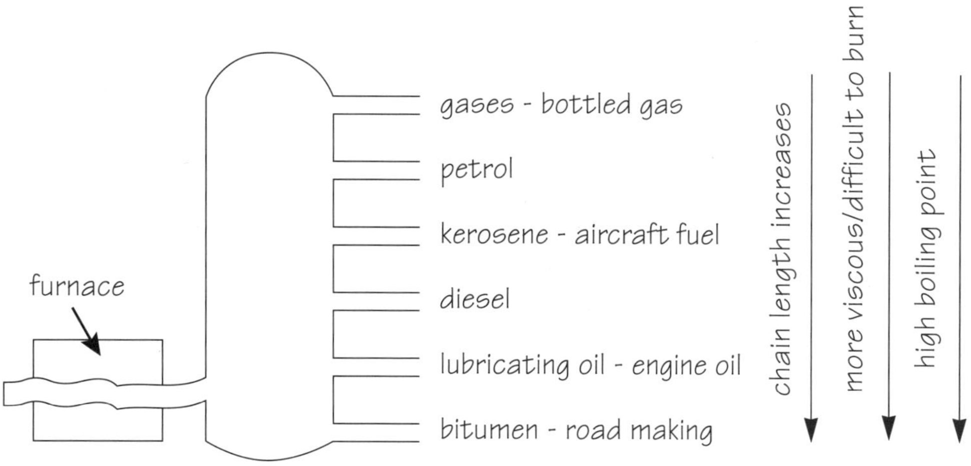

Key word **only**

- Crude oil contains **hydrocarbons**.
- Hydrocarbons contain **only hydrogen** and **carbon**.
- They **burn** in a **good** supply of air (oxygen) to form **carbon dioxide** and **water**.
- In a **limited** supply of air → **carbon monoxide** formed (**very poisonous**).

Saturated hydrocarbons → alkanes

- Molecules in which carbon atoms are linked by single **C-C covalent bonds**.

e.g. methane (g)

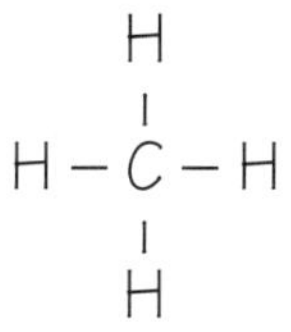

ethane (g)

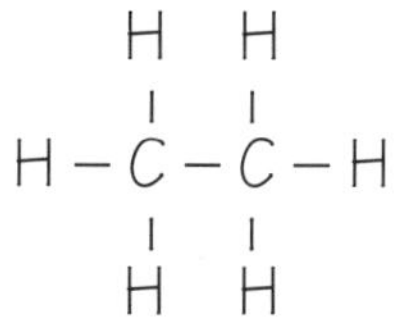

propane (g)

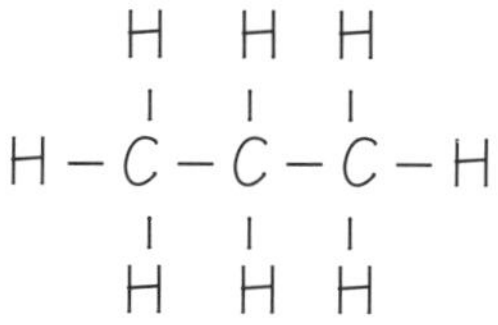

Unsaturated hydrocarbons → alkenes

- Molecules in which carbon atoms are linked by **double C=C bonds.**

e.g. ethene (g)

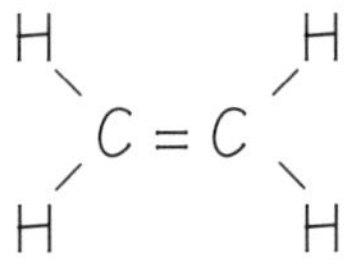

Test for single bonds – no colour change

propene (g)

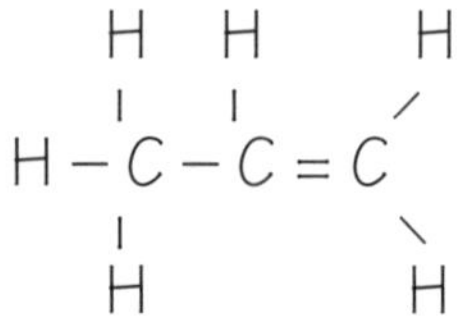

You must give the colour before and after the reaction

- React by breaking double bond and other atoms added on – **addition reactions** – bonds become single.

e.g.

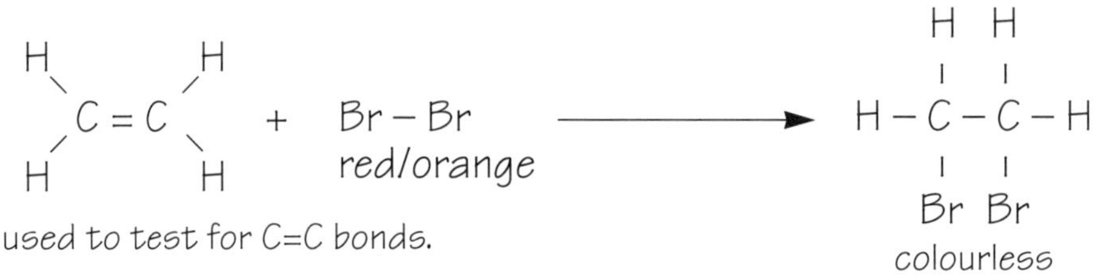

Br_2 – used to test for C=C bonds.

Cracking

Process in which large hydrocarbon molecules are **broken down** into **smaller, more useful molecules.**

e.g.

Word equation	decane	→	octane for petrol	+	ethene (to make polyethene)
Chemical equation	$C_{10}H_{22}$	→	C_8H_{18}	+	C_2H_4

Macromolecules

- Very large molecules which have very useful properties.

Two types:

- **Addition polymers** – **large number of small molecules** (**monomers**) **join together → polymer → process called polymerisation.**

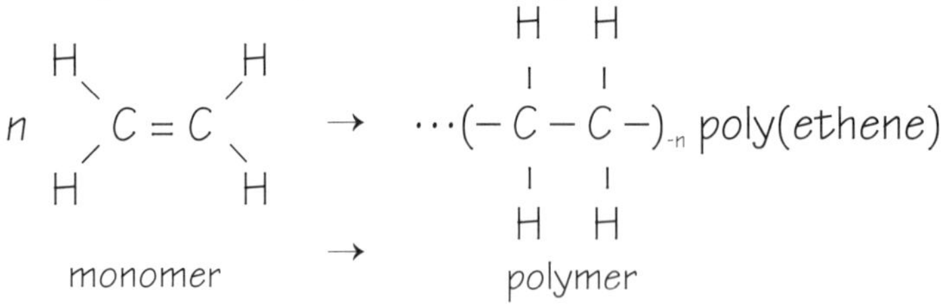

($n > 50$)

- **Condensation polymers** – **monomers join together to form a large chain and a small molecule,** e.g. water, **is given out.**

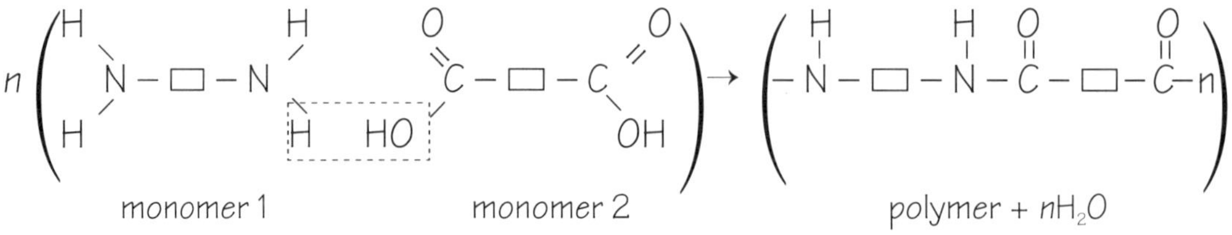

- **Synthetic** polymers e.g. nylon, polyester.
- **Natural** polymers e.g. starch (**monomer – glucose**), proteins (**monomers – amino acids**).

Materials & their properties

Questions

1 In an experiment it was found that 1.12 g of iron reacted with 2.13 g of chlorine. Calculate the formula of the compound formed (relative atomic mass: Fe = 56, Cl = 35.5).

____

____

____

____

2 A molten electrolyte contains sodium ions, Na^+ and chloride ions, Cl^-.

(**a**) Explain why the electrolyte conducts electricity.

____

____

(**b**) Chloride ions, Cl^-, react at the anode.

The equation for the reaction is: ______________________________

This is an example of oxidation. Explain why.

____

3 A hydrocarbon, propane (C3H8), was burned in a plentiful supply of air (oxygen).

(**a**) Write a word and a balanced chemical equation for the reaction.

word equation ______________________________

chemical equation ______________________________

(**b**) A hydrocarbon is a substance which contains____________and____________, ____________

(**c**) Crude oil can be__________into__________by the process of____________

4 The amount of carbon dioxide and oxygen in the atmosphere stays roughly constant.

Green plants take in__________and change it into food and__________.

This process is called__________. When fossil fuels are burned__________is used up.

5 Ammonia is formed from hydrogen and nitrogen.

$$N_2(g) + 3H_2(g) \rightleftharpoons 2NH_3(g) \quad \Delta H = -92 \text{ kJ/mol}$$

Explain how the equilibrium could be shifted to the left (increasing reactants).

____

____

Materials & their properties • Answers

Atomic structure

1 (**a**) 7, 3, (2, 1)
7, 3, 4, 2 (2)
6, 6 (2, 4)
7, 6 (2, 4)
20, 10 (2, 8)
16, 16, (2, 8, 8)
(**b**) Li^+, Ne and S^{2-}

2

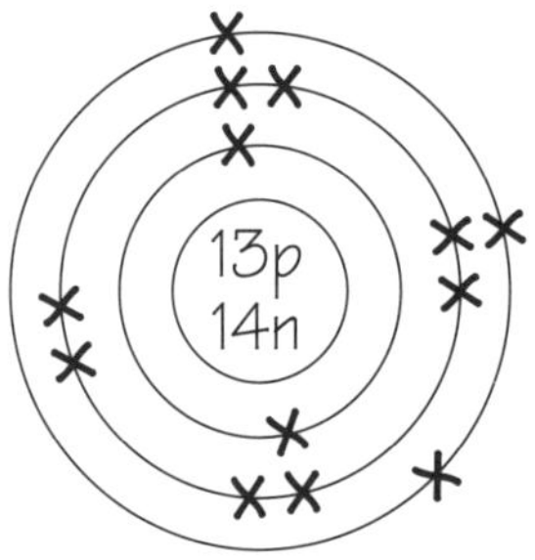

3

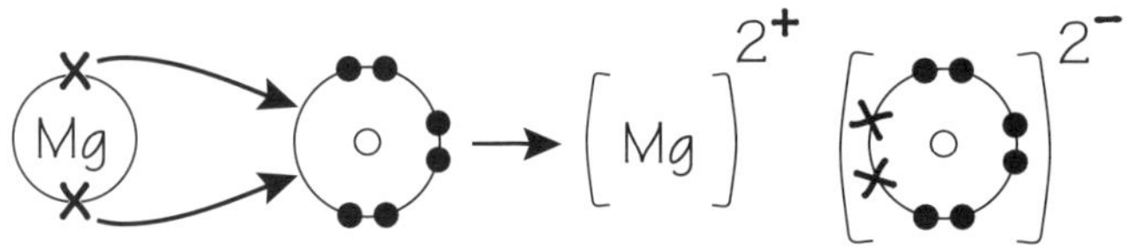

4 Protons, electrons

5 (**a**) A (**b**) C (**c**) B

Patterns of behaviour

1 (**a**) A/B/C/D (**b**) E (**c**) D (**d**) $2Ca + O_2 \rightarrow 2CaO$ **2** (**a**) Group 1, alkali metals, under oil, reacts, water (**b**) floats, moves on surface, fumes, cloudy solution **3** Haber process, ammonia **4** Noble gases, react, 8 (0) **5** Group VII, halogens $Cl_2 + 2Br^- \rightarrow 2Cl^- + Br_2$ displacement reaction **6** Hard, high density, catalysts **7** (**a**) Bromine (**b**) Sodium chloride (**c**) Silver bromide

Materials & their properties

1 mol Fe= 1.12/56 = 0.02 mol Cl= 2.13/35.5 = 0.06 Ratio Fe : Cl = 1 : 3, formula $FeCl_3$ **2** (**a**) Ions are free to move about. (**b**) $2Cl^- \rightarrow Cl_2 + 2e^-$ or $2Cl^- \rightarrow Cl_2 + 2e$ or $Cl^- \rightarrow Cl + e$ Electrons are being lost. **3** (**a**) propane + oxygen → carbon dioxide + water $C_3H_8 + 5O_2 \rightarrow 3CO_2 + 4H_2O$ (**b**) Hydrogen, carbon, only (**c**) Separated, fractions, fractional distillation **4** Carbon dioxide, oxygen, photosynthesis, oxygen **5** Any of following: increasing the temperature, decreasing the pressure, removing the reactants, adding more ammonia

Physical processes

Electricity & magnetism

Electrostatics

- **Static electricity** – electric charges **stationary**
- **Charges** – **positive** (+) or **negative** (–)
- **Insulators** – substances in which **electricity cannot flow** e.g. plastics
- **Conductors** – substances in which **electricity can flow** e.g. metals
- **Electron transfer** – two insulators rubbed together
- **Insulator** + **electrons** → **negative charge** (–)
- **Insulator** – **electrons** → **positive charge** (+)

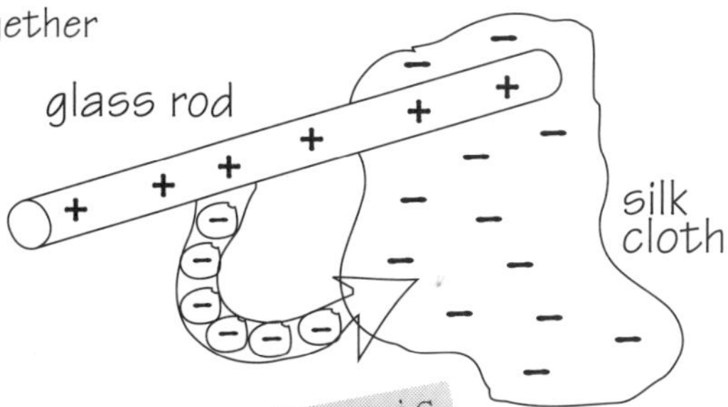

Charged Objects

- **Like charges repel** + and + or – and –
- **Unlike charges attract** + and –
- **Charged objects attract uncharged** objects

unlike magnetic poles also attract

Applications

You need to be able to describe advantages and disadvantages

Electrostatic filters – used to clean smoky chimneys
Aircraft fuel lines – earthed to avoid sparks/fire

Electrolysis

- **Ionic compounds** e.g. Sodium Chloride NaCl **conduct electricity** when molten or dissolved in water
- **Negative (–) ions flow to anode** (positive electrode)
- **Positive (+) ions flow to cathode** (negative electrode)
- **Substances deposited/released at electrodes**

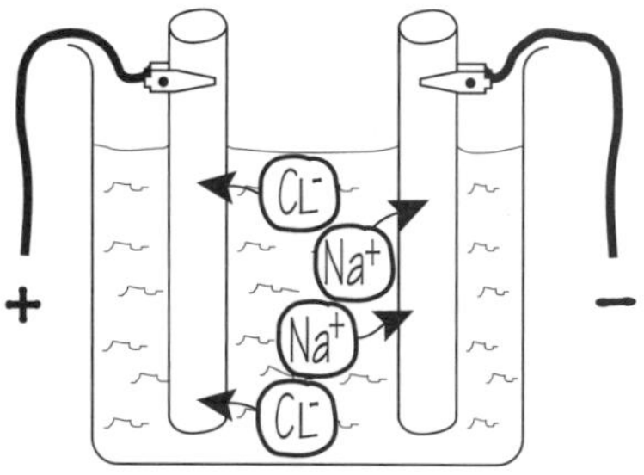

- **Amount of substance deposited/released greater when**
  - **the size of the current greater**
  - **the time for which the current flows greater**

Current Electricity

Resistance

- **Current electricity** – (negative) electric charges **move**
- **Resistance** – anything that **hinders movement**
- **Resistance of conductor greater** – conductor **longer or thinner**
  – conductor **hotter**
- **Resistance different** – **different materials** e.g. copper and lead
- **Ohm's law** – $\text{resistance} = \frac{\text{voltage}}{\text{current}}$
- **Units** – **ohms** (Ω)

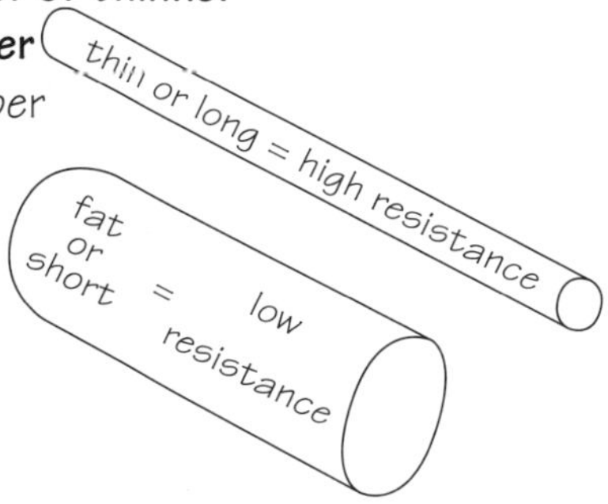

Graphs should have a label and unit on each axis

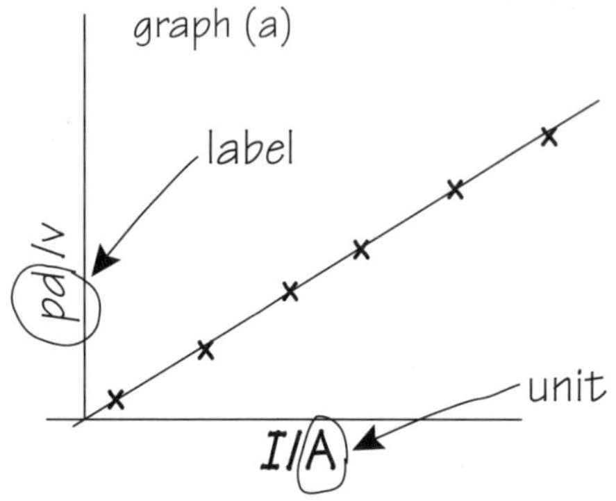

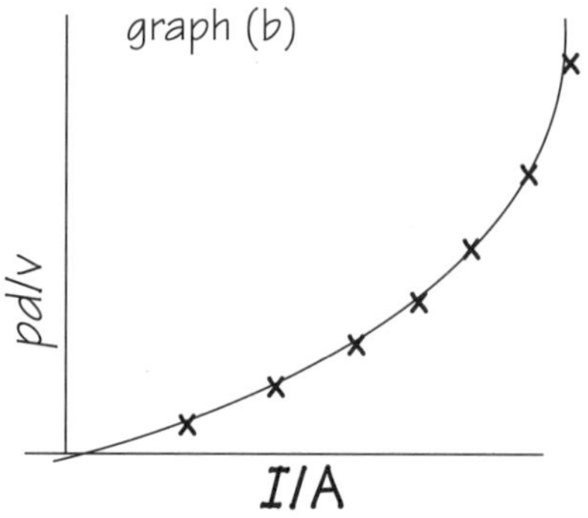

- **Ohmic conductor – resistance constant** (graph a) e.g. metal wire
- **Non–ohmic conductor – resistance varies** (graph b) e.g. lamp filament
- **Series resistors** $R = R_1 + R_2$
  - **current same**
  - **potential difference (pd) divided up**

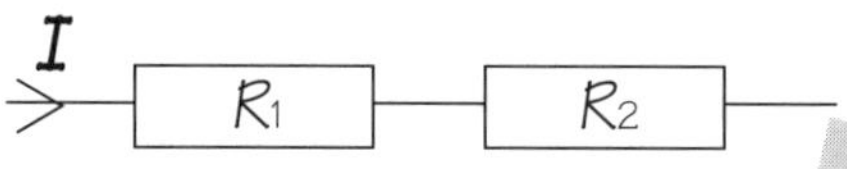

- **Parallel resistors** $\frac{1}{R} = \frac{1}{R_1} + \frac{1}{R_2}$
  - **current divided**
  - **pd same**

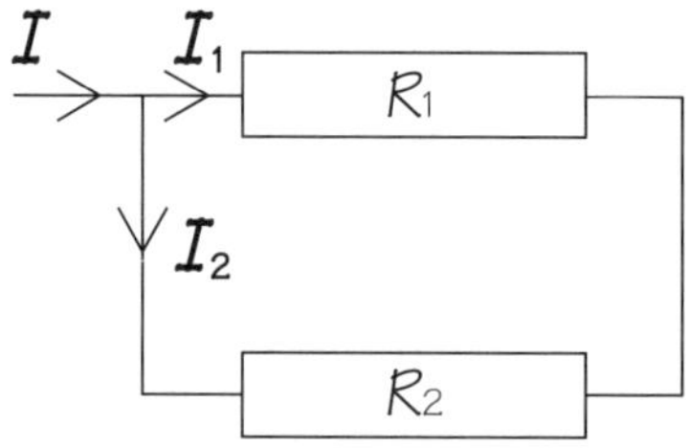

Note that 'I' is the symbol for current. 'A' stands for Amperes (Amps)

If $R_1 = R_2$, $R = R_1/2 = R_2/2$

Using electricity

Energy in circuits

- **Electric current – flow of charge**
- **Energy – given to each electron** by battery/power supply
- **More energy – (pd) higher**
- **1 V – 1 J per coulomb of charge (C)**
- **1 A – current when 1 C flows/second**
- **Energy transfer – Power = pd x current**
  = energy transfer/second
- **Units of power – 1W = 1J/s**

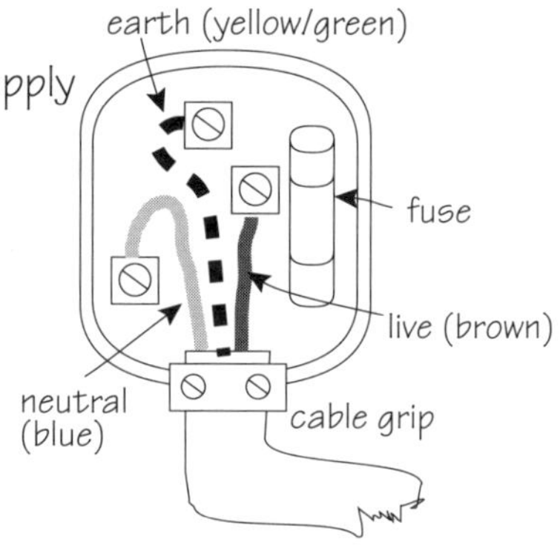

Safety

There is usually a question on plugs and/or fuses

- **Fuse – low melting-point wir**e.
- **Plug** – 3-pin plug needs **correct fuse**
- **Fuse size** – use I = P V where p is the power rating in Watts
- **High current** e.g. 12 A – **large fuse,** 13 A
- **Low current** e.g. 1 A – **small fuse,** 2 A
- **Circuit breaker – instead of fuse**
- **Metal** case – **appliance must be earthed**
- **Plastic** case – **extra protection**

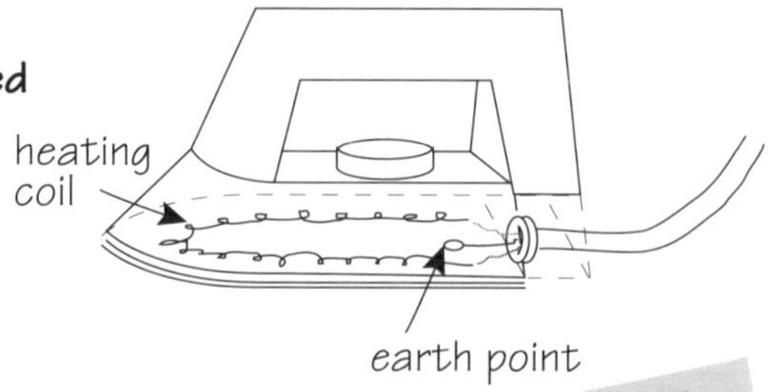

If live wire loose large current -> earth

Cost

- **Unit – kilowatt hour (kWh)**
- **Kilowatt – 1000 watts**
- **Total cost –** number of units x cost per unit
- **Example** – 3 kW for 3 hours = 9 units
  9 units @ 6p = 54p

Electromagnetism

Note that it behaves like a bar magnet

Electromagnets

- **Electromagnet – coil of wire with electric current**
- **Strength** of an electromagnet **increased by**
  - placing an **iron core** in it
  - **increasing the number of turns of wire**
  - **increasing size of current** through it

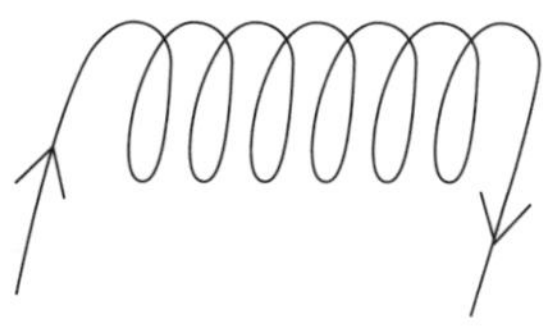

Electromagnetic forces

- **Force on wire in magnetic field**
- **Direction of force –**
  - Fleming's **Left Hand Rule**
  - **direction** of force **reverses** if **current reverses**
- **Size of force increases with**
  - strength of **magnetic field**
  - size of **current**
  - increased **number of turns of wire**

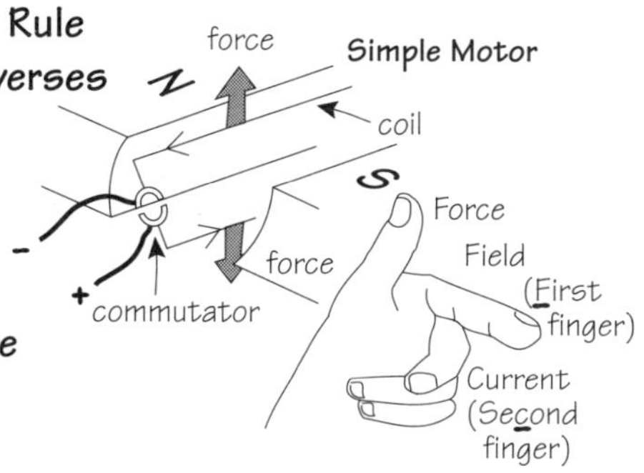

Applications

- **Motors** – force produces **rotary movement** e.g. electric drill, washing machine
- **Loudspeakers** – **cone forced in and out** to produce sound waves
- **Circuit breakers – high current activates electromagnet**

Examiners often set questions on applications to show an understanding of the principles

Electromagnetic induction

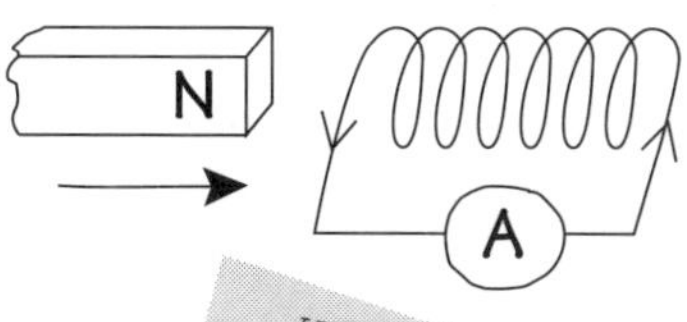

- **Magnet —> coil of wire – current induced**
- **Coil of wire —> magnet – current induced**
- **No movement – no current**

Use the right hand rule to find the direction of the current in a generator

Applications

- **Generator/dynamo – produces electricity**
- **Transformers** (see below) – **change size** of a **voltage**

Alternating current

- **Direct current** (dc) – **electrons move in one direction**
- **Batteries produce dc**
- **Alternating current** (ac) – **electrons change direction**
- **Power stations produce ac**

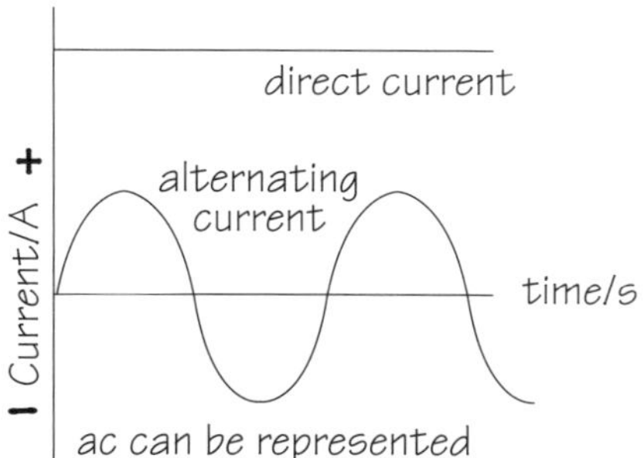

ac can be represented graphically by a sine wave

Transformers

- **High current** – a lot of **heat**
- **High voltage – avoid heat loss**
- **Power stations** – produce electricity at **high voltage**
- **Transformers – step down** (or **up**) **voltages**
  - **work on ac not dc**
- **Electricity at home – 240 V ac** (in UK)

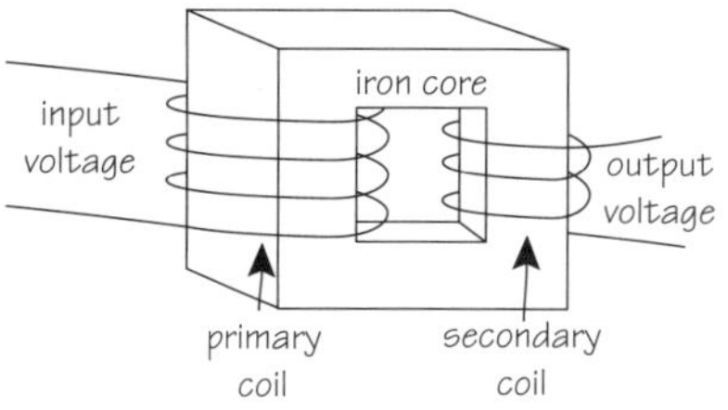

secondary pd = primary pd × no. secondary turns/no. primary turns

Control in electronic circuits

Electronic systems

- **Input sensors – detect change** e.g. LDR's (light), thermistors (heat)
- **Processor – decides action** needed e.g. logic gates **AND, OR, NOT**
- **Output devices – indicate result** of action e.g. buzzer

Logic gates

- **Process information**
- **Output current – too small** to operate most output devices
- **Output – predicted** from '**truth table**'
- **AND** – output if **both inputs** high
- **OR** – output if **one input** high
- **NOT – output reversed**

The NOT gate reverses the input to the transistor

Variable resistor used to adjust sensitivity of circuit

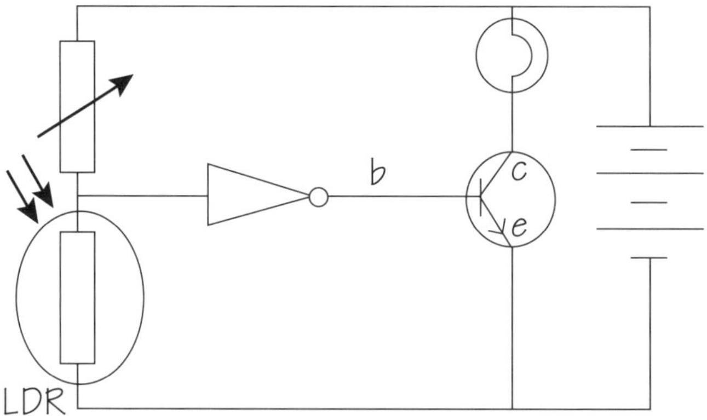

Potential divider

- **Divides up pd**
- **Series components** – divide up pd
- **Provides correct output**

Transistor

- **Three terminals** – base (b)
  – collector (c)
  – emitter (e)
- **Acts as – switch**
  – current amplifier
- **Switched on – large enough current** to base
- **Switched off – no/too little current** to base

light level drops ——> transistors switches on

Capacitor

Capacitors are often used as time delay switches in an electronic circuit

- **Two metal plates + insulator**
- **Stores charge** – connected across power supply
- **Discharges** – conductor connected across it
- **Time to charge/discharge depends on**
  – resistance
  – capacitance

Electricty & magnetism
Questions

1 In terms of charge transfer, describe what happens when you rub a glass rod with a silk cloth. ______

______

2 In this circuit, the two lamps are identical.

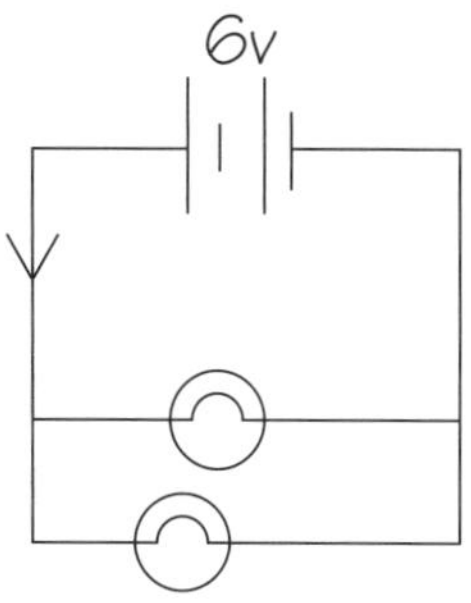

a) What is the pd across each lamp? ____ V

b) If the current flow in the main part of the circuit is 3.0A, calculate the resistance of each lamp filament.

______

______

c) Why might your answer be inaccurate? ______

______

3 An electric kettle is rated at 1.5 kW.

a) Assuming that the domestic voltage supply is 250 V, what is the correct-sized fuse for the plug? (Choose from the following sizes: 1 A, 2 A, 3 A, 5 A, 10 A, 13 A) ______

______

b) A unit of electricity costs 6p. How much does it cost to operate the kettle each day for a week, 20 minutes a day? ______

______

4 a) What is meant by a step-up transformer? ______

______

b) The primary coil of a transformer has 100 turns. A pd of 2.0 V is applied across it. If an output voltage of 7.0 V is needed, how many turns of wire should the secondary coil have? ______

______

5 a) In this circuit, the resistor, R and the thermistor, T form a 'potential divider'. Explain what this means.

______

______

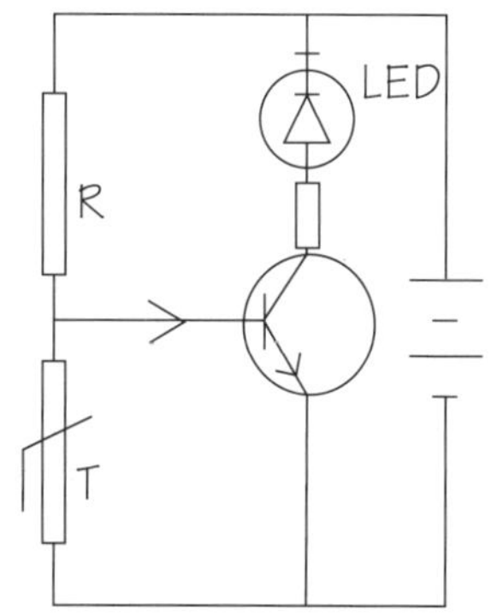

b) The resistance of the thermistor decreases when it gets hotter. What then happens in the rest of the circuit as the thermistor is heated?

______

______

Forces & motion

Representing motion

Distance – time graphs

- **Speed = distance/time**
- **Units – m/s** (ms^{-1})
- ***Graph a* – stationary** body
- ***Graphs b* and *c* – steady** speed
- **Gradient —> speed**
- ***b* faster than *c***

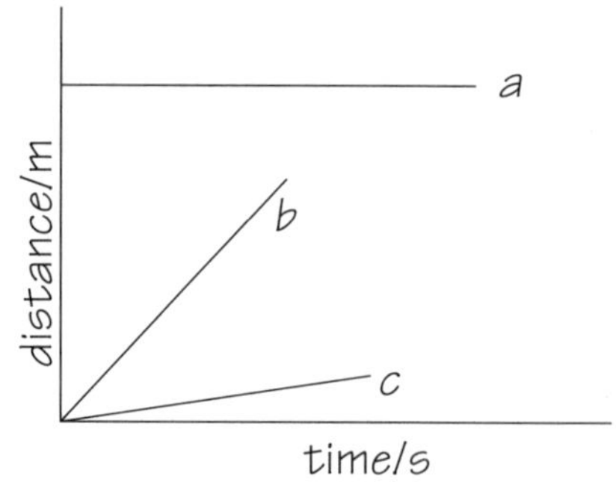

Velocity – time graphs

- **Acceleration = change in velocity/time taken**

Examiners usually set questions on drawing or interpreting graphs

- **Units – m/s²** (ms^{-2})
- ***Graph a* – constant velocity**
- ***Graphs b* and *c* – constant acceleration**
- **Gradient —> acceleration**
- ***b* greater acceleration than *c***

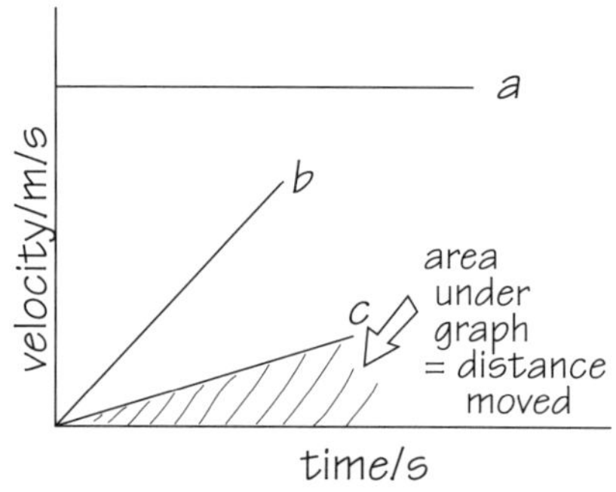

Force – extension graphs

- **Linear part** – $F \propto e$ (Hooke's Law)
- ***OA* – elastic** region
- ***AB* – plastic** region
- ***B* – yield point;** wire stretches with little load
- ***C* – breaking point**

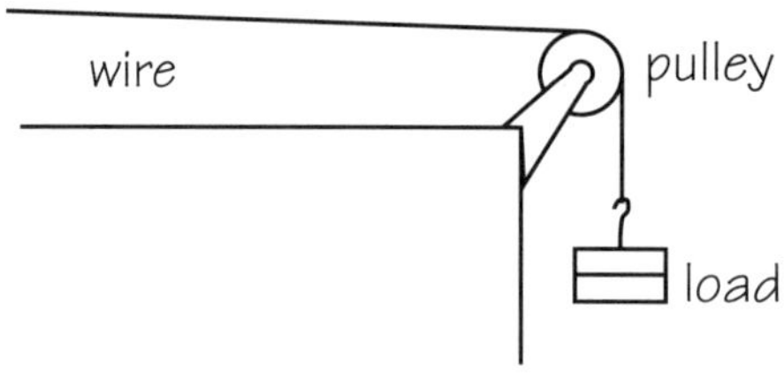

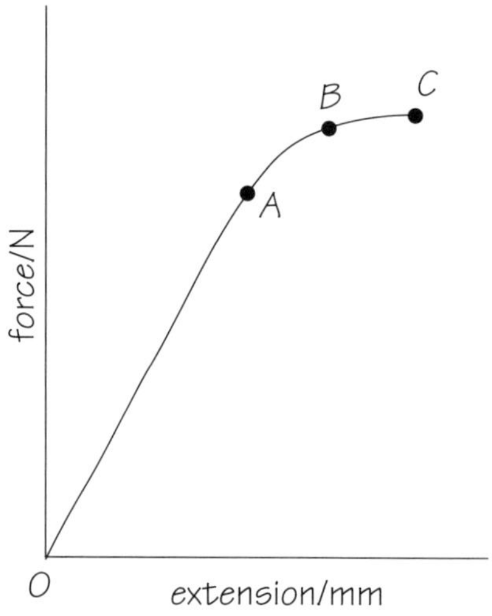

Balanced forces

- **Weight, *W* – downwards** on table
- **Force, *R* – upwards** on book
- ***R* = *W* – forces balance**
  – book **stationary**

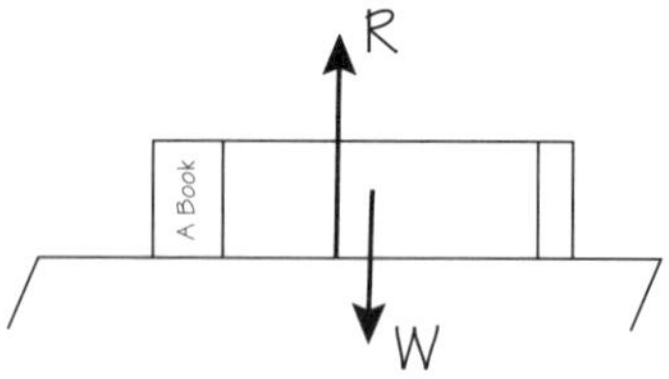

- **Thrust, *T* – car pushed through air**
- **Force, *R* – air drag** on car
- ***R* = *T* – forces balance**
  – car **constant speed**

other (frictional) forces also act on the car

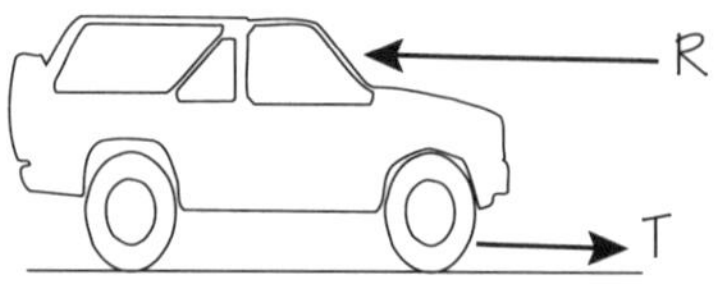

- ***W* greater than *R* —> book falls!**

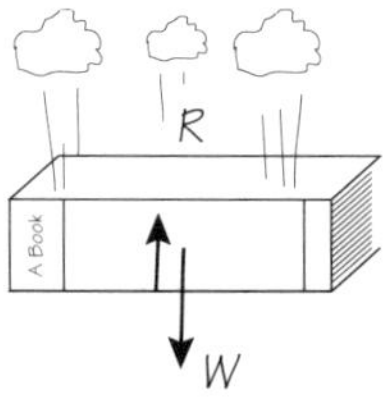

- ***T* greater than *R* —> car accelerates!**
- **Forces unbalanced**
- **Unbalanced forces – change in motion**
- **Force = mass × acceleration**
- **Units – Newtons (N)**
- **1 N – 1 kg m/s²**

Friction

You need to be able to state or describe both advantages and disadvantages

- **Friction acts**
  - between two **surfaces that move**
  - when **body moves through gas or liquid**
- **Friction** – **opposes motion**
  - causes **heating/wear** e.g. car engine
  - **needed** for moving and stopping

Road safety

- **Stopping distance depends on**
  - driver **reaction time**
  - **braking distance**
- **Braking distance depends on**
  - **speed**
  - **tyres**
  - **brakes**
  - **road surface**

These data are found on back cover of the Highway Code

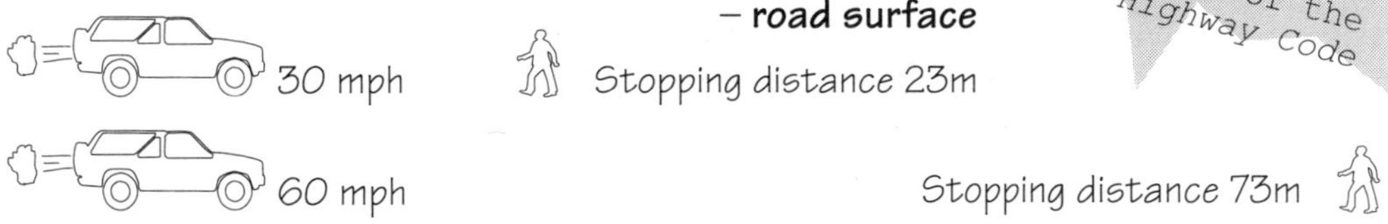

Free fall

- **Weight** —> **acceleration**
- **Air drag, *R*** – **increases** with speed
- ***R* = *W*** —> terminal velocity
- **Terminal velocity** – **constant**
  - **zero acceleration**
  - about **170 mph** in air

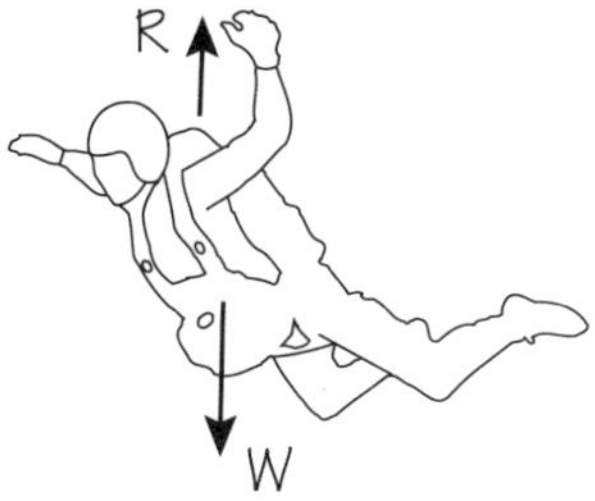

Turning forces

- **Weight** – **windmill turns**
- **Turning effect greater if**
  - **weight** (or force) **greater**
  - **distance** to pivot is **greater**
- **Turning effect** = **force** X **perpendicular distance to pivot**
- **Moment** – another name for **turning effect**

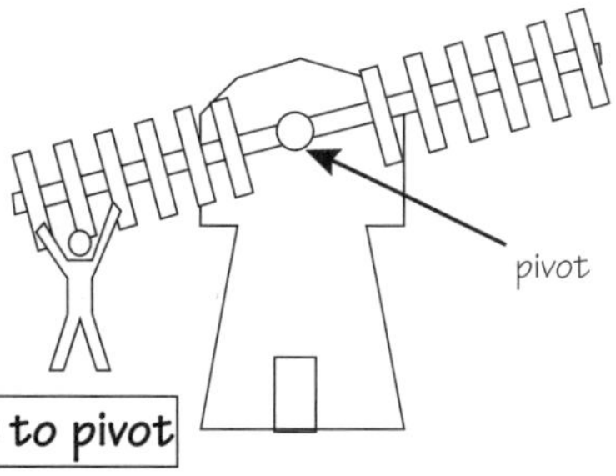

- **Centre of mass** – where body **balances**
- **LH force/s** – turn beam ↶
- **RH force/s** – turn beam ↷
- **balance** – ↶ **moments** = ↷ **moments**

Words clockwise and anticlockwise don't need to appear if symbols ↶ and ↷ do

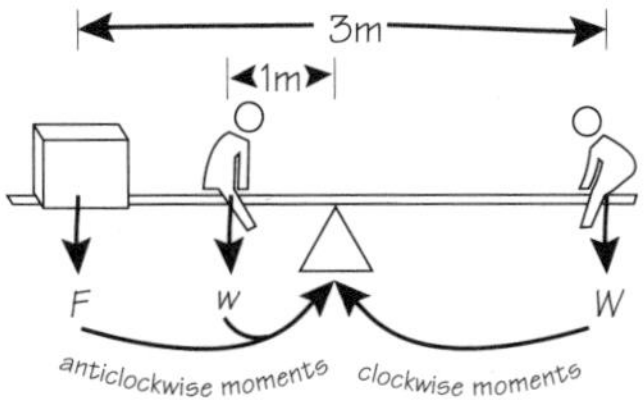

$F \times 1.5 + w \times 1 = W \times 1.5$

- **Stable** – **weight line inside base**
- **Unstable** – **falls** if pushed
  - **weight line outside base**
- **Neutral** – **centre of mass stays same height**

Stability increases if centre of mass is nearer ground e.g. sports car

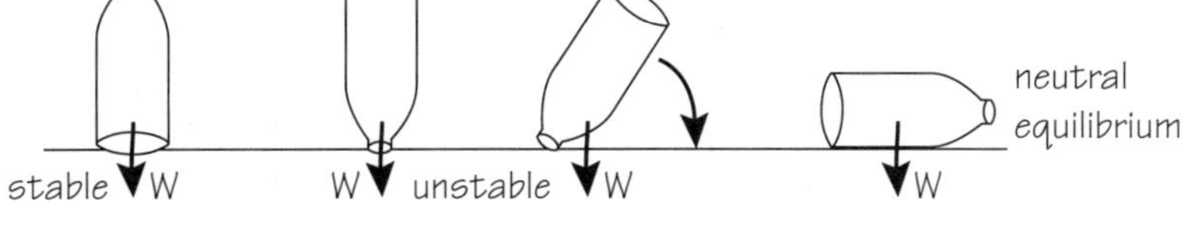

Momentum

Remember to quote correct units in a calculation

- **Momentum = mass × velocity**
- **Units – kg m/s**
- **Collision/explosion – –ve force = +ve force**
  —> momentum change
- **Conservation – momentum before = momentum after**
  – **KE usually less after collision** —> heat/sound

Planetary orbits are not perfectly circular; they are elliptical

Circular motion

Stability

- **Circular path – direction changes** —> **velocity changes** —> **acceleration**
- **Centripetal force** – acts on body since **$f = m \times a$**
  – acts **towards centre**
- **Centripetal force greater if**
  – **mass** of body **greater**
  – **speed** of body **greater**
  – **radius** of circle **smaller**
- **Examples – planetary motion**/motion of **satellites**
  – **car rounding a bend**

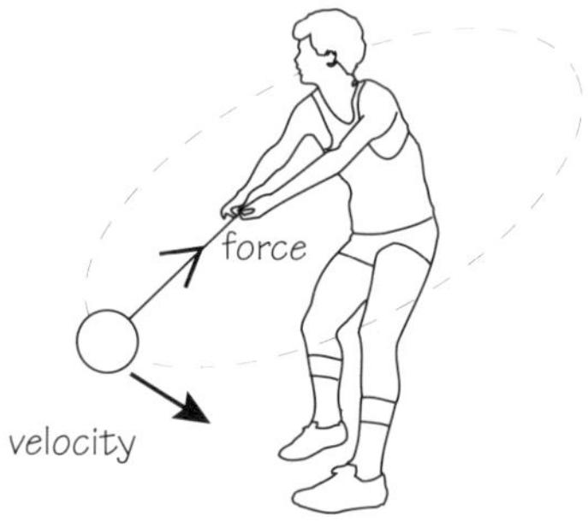

Pressure

Solids

- **Pressure = force/area**
- **Units – N/m^2**
- **1 N/m^2 = 1 pascal (Pa)**
- **Stiletto heel – small area**
- **Small area —> high pressure**
- **Snow skis – large area**
- **Large area —> low pressure**

Example of high pressure

Example of low pressure

Liquids

- **Pressure = $d \times h \times g$**
- **d – density**
- **h – depth**
- **g – gravitational field strength** (10 N/kg)
- **Pressure – equal** in all directions

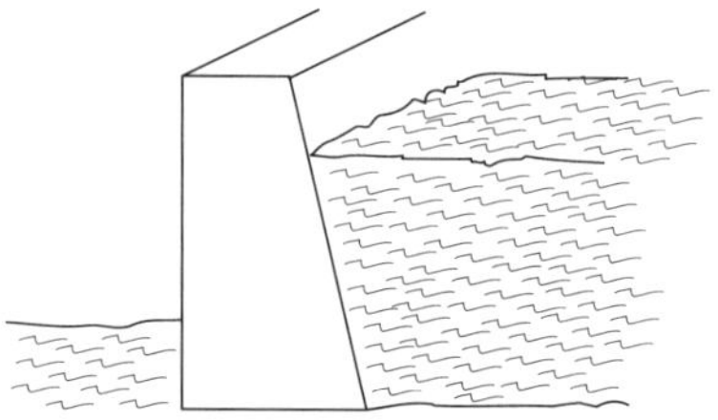

A dam is thicker at its base

Example:
- **Hydraulic system** – e.g. car jack, car brakes
- **Master piston A – transmits pressure** A
- **Brake piston B – pressed** by liquid B
  – has **larger area**
- **$P = F/A$ —> force α area**
- **Force exerted – larger**
  – **magnified by ratio of area B/area A**

this is the important bit to remember in calculations

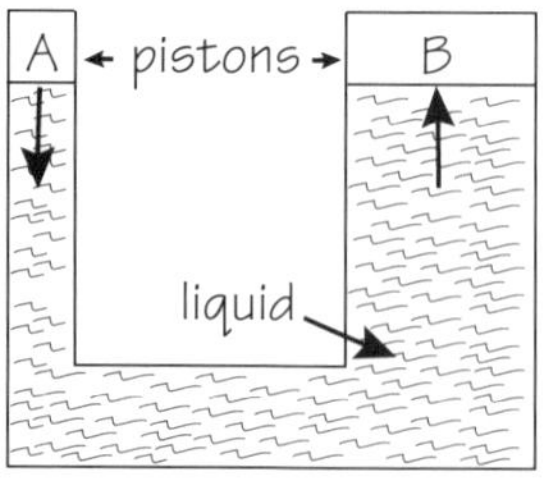

Gases

You should be able to explain gas pressure in terms of particles colliding with container walls

- **Volume** of gas – **decreases** when **pressure increases**
- **Temperature** – constant
- **Mathematically – V α 1/p** —> Boyle's Law

- Example –
  bicycle pump – press on piston
  – volume of air decreases

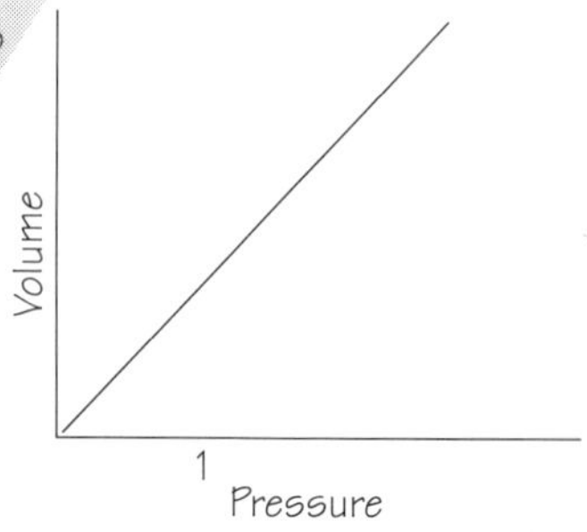

Forces & Motion

Questions

1 A lorry starts from rest. A velocity–time graph of its motion is drawn for the first 30 seconds.

a) Describe its motion ____________________

____

b) Calculate

i) its acceleration ____________________

____

ii) the distance moved ____________________

____

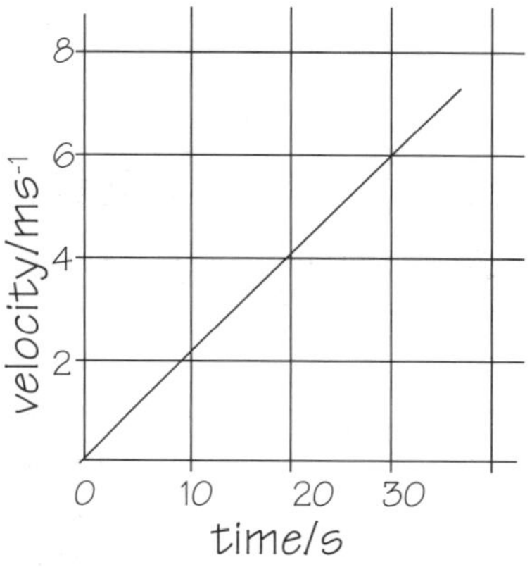

2 The mass of a sports car is 1200 kg. The engine provides a thrust of 6500 N. Over a measured course, the average air drag is found to be 850 N.

a) What acceleration is produced? ____________________

____

b) What does the total stopping distance depend upon? ____________________

____

3 A uniform beam of length 2.5 m is used to weigh sacks of flour. A weight of 120 N has to be placed at point X for it to balance. X is 1/5 of the beam's length from the pivot. What is the weight of the flour? ____________________

____

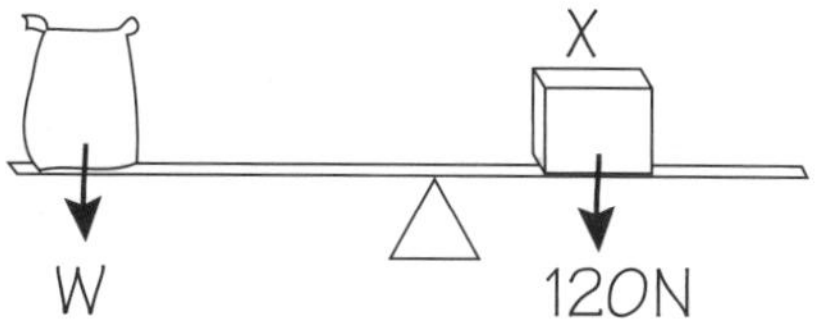

4 Bus A of mass 5000 kg is travelling east at 10 m/s. At the same time, bus B of mass 3000 kg is travelling in the same direction at 5 m/s. When they collide A and B move together as one. At what speed will they continue to move?

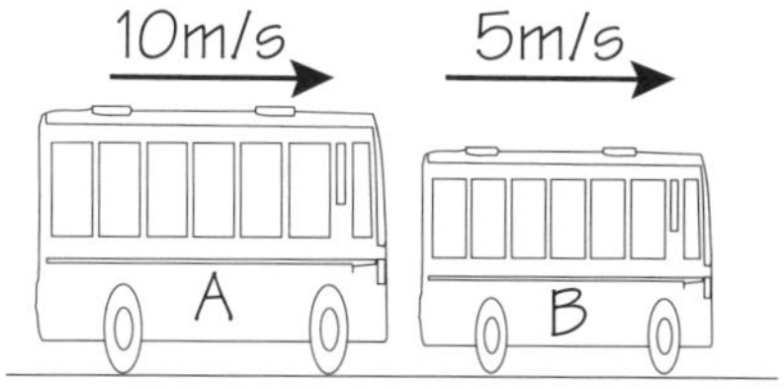

____

____

____

5 In a car brake system, the brake pedal pushes on a master piston of area 0.1 m^2 with a force of 150 N. If the brake piston is of area 0.4 m^2, what force is exerted on the wheels to stop them?

____

____

Waves

- **Waves transfer energy** not matter

Transverse waves

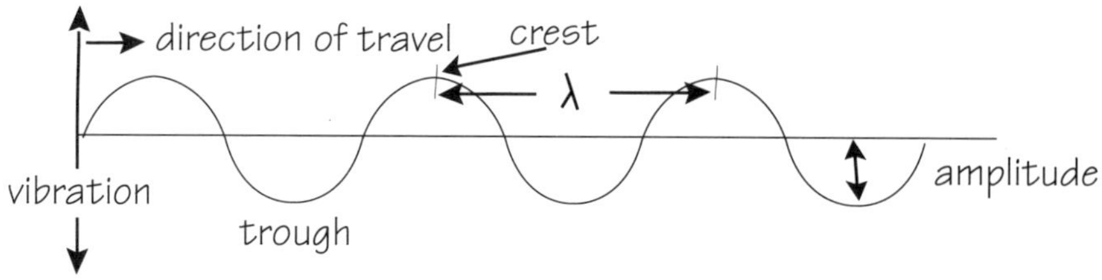

- **Examples – water, light, radio**
- **Vibration – 90° to direction of travel**
- **Wavelength** (λ) – from **one crest to the next**
- **Frequency – number of waves per second**; 1 Hz = 1 wave/sec
- **Electromagnetic waves** e.g. light **can travel in a vacuum**

Longitudinal wave

- **Examples – sound, slinky** spring as diagram below
- **Vibration – same direction as travel**
- **Wavelength** – from **one compression to the next**
- **Sound travels in solids, liquids, gases but not a vacuum**

Often, questions on sound waves will show them looking like transverse waves

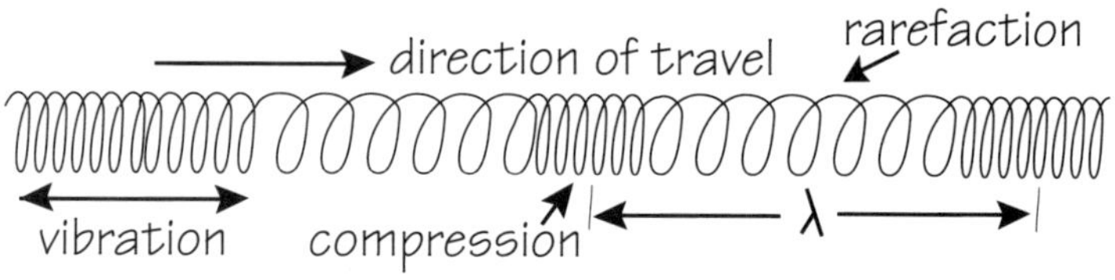

- **Wavespeed = wavelength × frequency** ; $v = \lambda \times f$

Properties of waves

Reflection

Remember arrows on diagram show direction of the light

- **Angle *i* = angle *r* for all waves**
- **Mirror image – virtual**
  - – same size
  - – upright
  - – OM = MI

A quick way to draw this accurately:-
1) draw object + 2 incident rays
2) since OM = MI, draw in image
3) draw dotted lines joining incident rays to image
4) extend dotted lines as rays on LH side of mirror

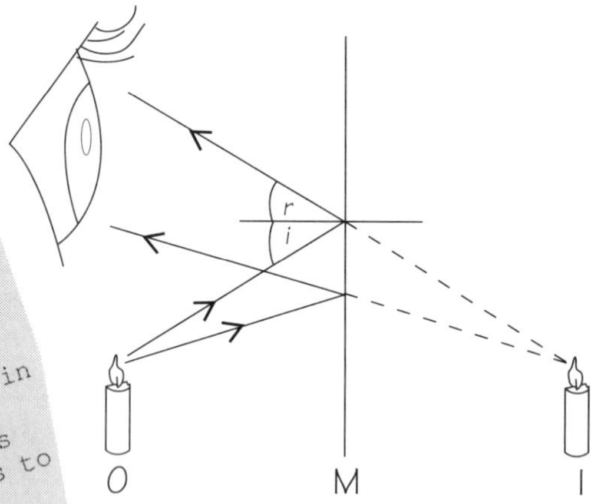

Refraction

Emergent ray is parallel to incident ray

- **Less dense to more dense – direction changes**
- **Direction at A – towards normal**
- **Direction at B – away from normal**
- **Denser medium – greater refraction**
- **Refractive index – measure of refraction**
  - **– sin *i*/sin *r***
  - **– about 1.5 for glass**
- **Example – bottom of swimming pool appears nearer**

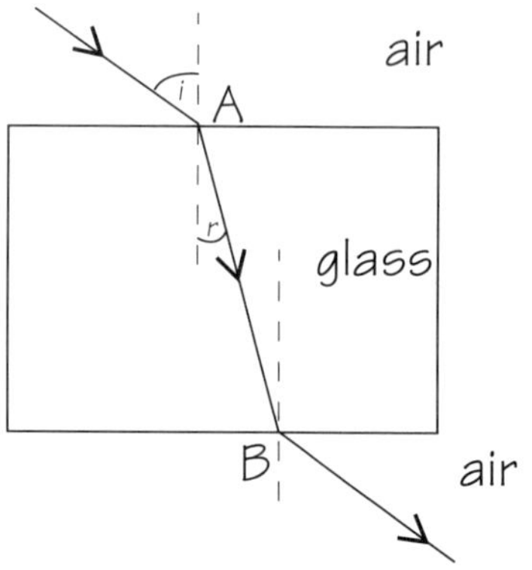

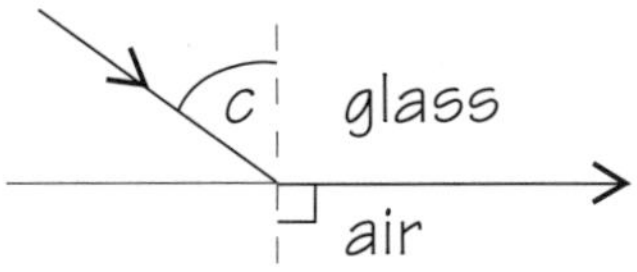

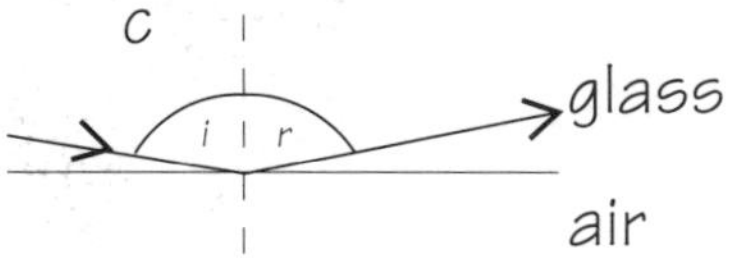

- Critical angle – light refracted at 90°

Note that this only occurs moving from more dense to less dense

- Incident angle greater – all light reflected back
- This is called **total internal reflection** (TIR)
- Example – optical fibre

Deffraction

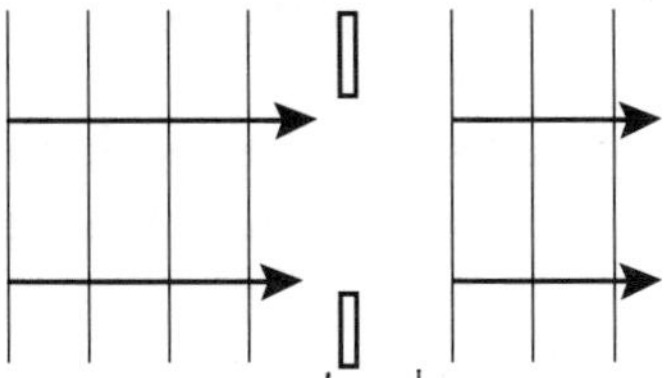

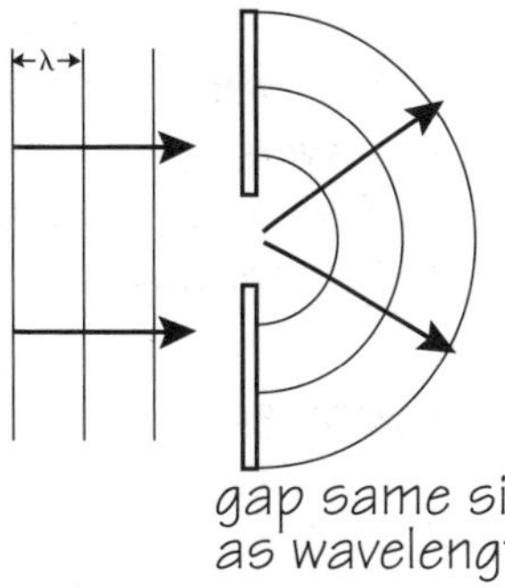

- Waves spread out – past obstacle/through gap
- Gap size – about same as wavelength
- Examples – sound heard around corners
  – radio signals received in shadow of hills

Electromagnetic spectrum

A mnemonic such as *Reading Is Lousy Unless Extremely Good* will help to remember the order

waveform decreases →   ← frequency increases

	Radio	Infra-red	Light	Ultra-violet	X-rays	Gamma-rays
Source	Vibrating electrons	Sun Hot bodies	Sun Luminous objects	Sun Mercury Vapour lamp	Stars X-ray tube	Radioactive substances
Detector	Radio aerial	Skin IR photographic film	Eye Photographic film	Skin (tanning) Photographic film	Photographic film	GM tube Photographic film
Use	Communication Cooking (microwaves)	Heating Remote control	Seeing Photography Photosynthesis	Security marking Fluorescent lamps	Medical photographs Astronomy	Cancer treatment

- Family of waves
- Speed – same = 3×10^{8} m s^{-1}
- Different wavelengths – reflected, refracted, etc. differently

Light

Students often do not show the red and violet rays spreading out from point A.

- **White light** – split into **colours** by prism
- **Spectrum – colour depends on wavelength**
- **Most refracted – red**
- **Least refracted – violet**
- **Brightness – depends on intensity/amplitude** of wave

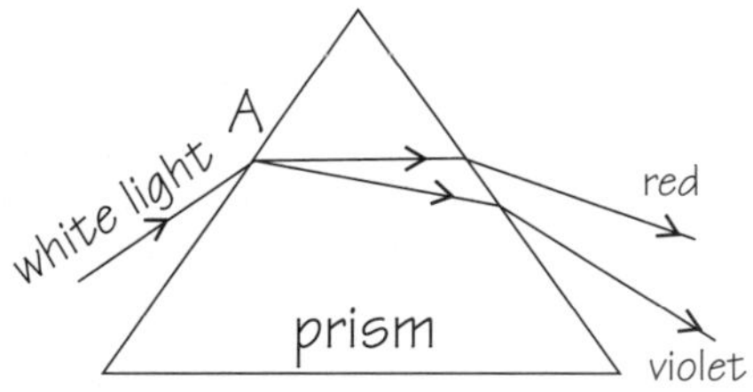

Using light

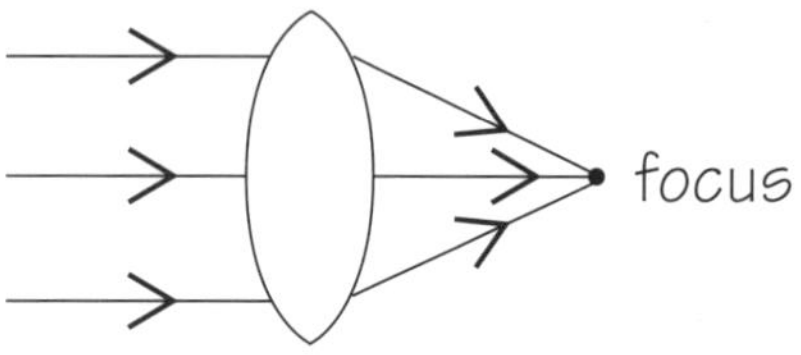

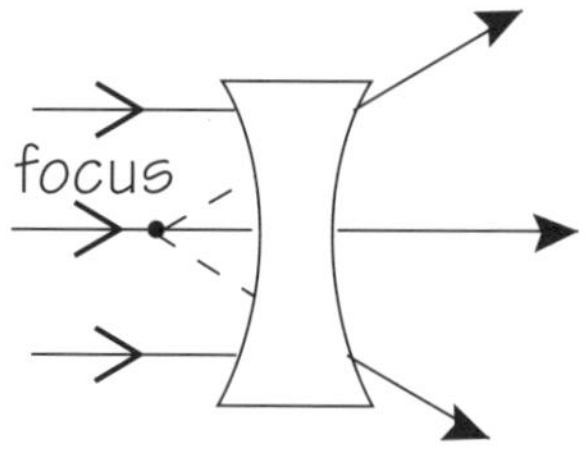

1 Convex lens
- **Focus – real;** parallel light converges
- **Real image** formed
- **Examples – eye, camera, magnifier**

2 Concave lens
- **Focus – virtual;** light spreads out
- **Virtual image formed**
- **Example – spectacle lens** (short sight)

3 Eye
- **Cornea/lens – focus** light
- **Image – inverted/smaller**
- **Thicker lens – converges** light **more**
- **Far objects – lens thinner**
- **Perfect eye** – light **focused on retina**
- **Ciliary muscles** – control **lens shape**
- **Near objects – light sensitive layer**
- **Retina – lens thicker**

Eye defects
- **Clouded cornea – replace** with clear plastic
- **Short sight – eye too long**/lens too thick
- – **correct** with **concave lens**
- **Long sight – eye too short**/lens too thin
  – **correct** with **convex lens**

The eye is similar in many ways to a simple camera

Questions are often set on eye defects

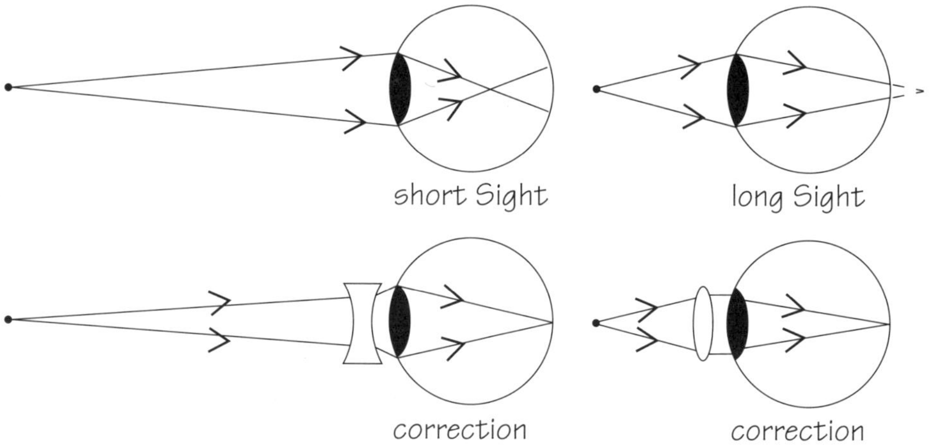

Sound

These are patterns seen on an oscilloscope

- **Vibration produces sound**
- **Examples** – guitar **string,** drum **skin, whistle**
- **Volume – depends on amplitude**
- **Pitch – depends on frequency**
- **Speed** – in **air** about **340 m/s**
  – **faster in denser** substances e.g. water
  – **measure by timing echoes**

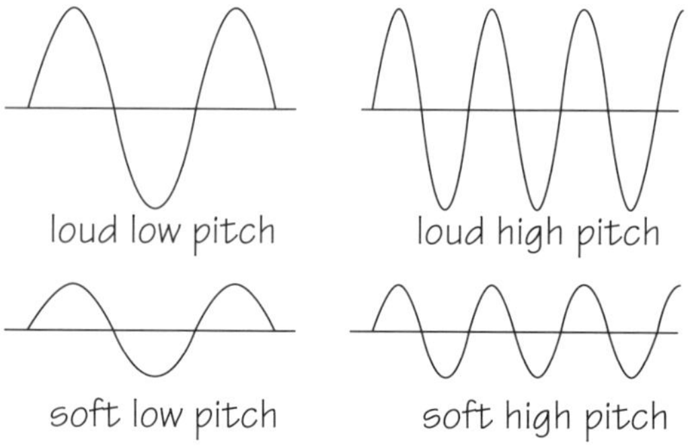

Using sound

1 Ear

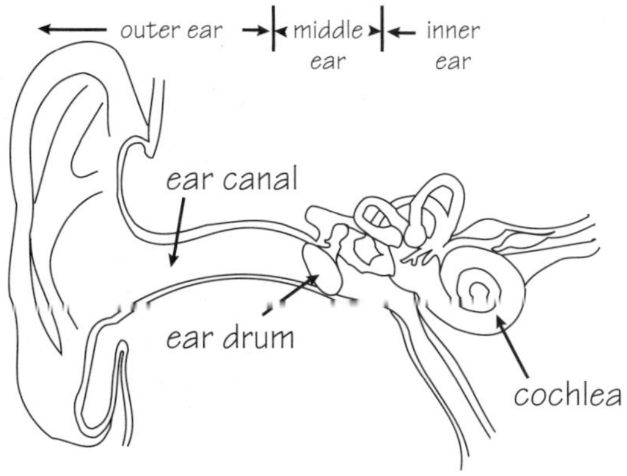

- Hearing range – up to 20 kHz in humans
  – dogs hear sounds above 20kHz
- Ear drum – vibrates
- Middle ear – bones vibrate
- Inner ear – liquid in cochlea vibrates

2 Ultrasound

- Definition – above 20 kHz
- Reflection – at boundary between media
  – time for detection gives distance
- Bats – detect objects from echoes
- Sea – measure depth
  – detect fish shoals
- Industry – cleaning delicate objects
  – detect flaws in metal casings
- Hospital – pre-natal scanning

dolphins produce ultra-sonic waves

Ultrasonic Scanning is thought to be safer than using X-rays; state this as a main advantage in an answer

3 Seismic waves – earthquakes

- P waves – longitudinal
  – fast
  – travel through solids, liquids
- S waves – transverse
  – slower
  – only travel through solids
- Refraction – at boundary between media
  – indicates changing density

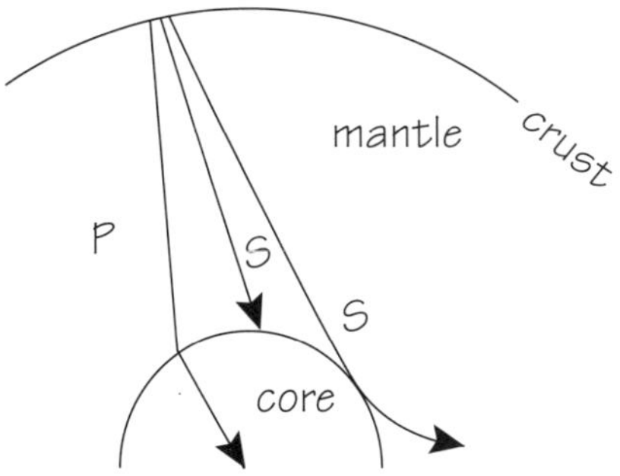

Observations suggest Earth – made of layers
– has thin crust
– has solid mantle with density increasing with depth
– has core just over half Earth diameter
– has core with liquid outer and solid inner part

S-waves cannot pass through dense core

Waves
Questions

1 Here is a waveform that you may see on an oscilloscope screen.

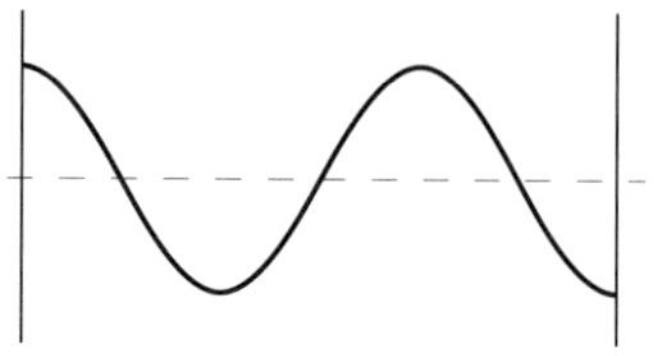

a) Measure i) its wavelength ________cm
ii) its amplitude ________cm

b) It takes 0.01 s for this waveform to travel across the screen.
Calculate i) its frequency ________________

ii) its speed ________________

2 a) Copy and complete the diagram to show how an image is formed in a plane mirror.

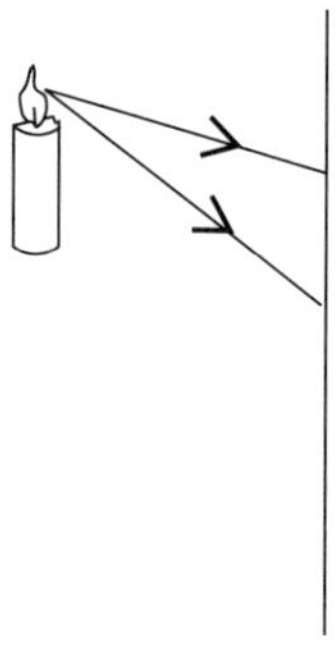

b) Is the image 'real' or 'virtual'? Explain your answer. ________________

3 Echo location techniques can be used by a fishing trawler to find shoals of fish in the sea. a) Describe how this works. ________________

b) If the speed of sound in water is 1550 m/s and it takes 0.3 s for an echo to be received, how deep is the shoal? ________________

4 Name two differences between P and S waves sent out from the epicentre of an earthquake. i) ________________
ii) ________________

The Earth & beyond
The Solar System

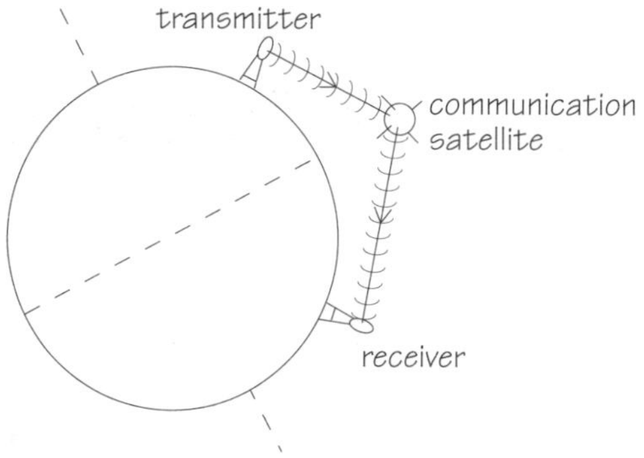

Satellites

There may well be a question on uses of satellites

- **Moon** – **natural satellite**
- **Sputnik** – *example of* **artificial satellite**
  – USSR 1957
- **Use** – **beam information** to places on Earth a long way apart, e.g. TV
  – **monitor conditions** etc. on Earth, e.g. weather
  – **acts as observatory** since no interference from atmosphere
- **Orbits** – **communication** satellite uses **high equatorial** orbit; scans same point continuously
  – **monitoring** satellite uses **low polar** orbit; scans whole N or S hemisphere each day

Orbit of communication satellite is "geostationary". Speed of rotation same as Earth

Gravity

- **Attraction** – **all bodies in Universe**
- **Gravitational force (*g*) greater if**
  – **mass** of bodies **greater**
  – **distance** apart **less**
- **Earth** – ***g*** **= 10 N/kg**
- **Larger planets** e.g. Jupiter – ***g*** **greater**
- **Smaller planets** e.g. Mercury – ***g*** **smaller**
- **Weightlessness** – **no weight**
  – **orbiting satellite**
  – **far out in space**

An apple weighs about 1 Newton!

Orbital motion

- **Planetary orbits** – **elliptical** not circular
- **Comets** – orbit **very elliptical**
  – much closer to Sun at times —> visible
- **Orbit larger** – **further** from Sun
  – **longer time** for orbit
- **Small bodies** e.g. satellites – **need certain speed** to stay in orbit

Note that the orbit of Pluto is at an angle to those of the other planets

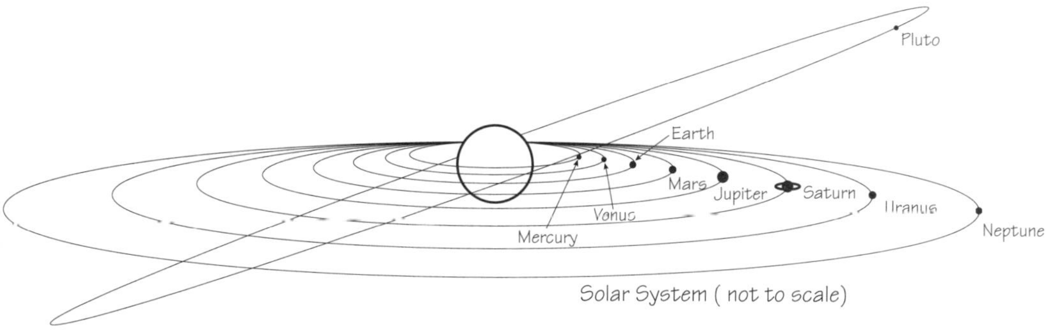

Solar System (not to scale)

Universe

Stars

- **Sun – one of millions of stars**
- **Galaxy – group of stars**
  – stars millions of times further apart than planets from Sun
- **Universe – at least one thousand million (billion) galaxies**
  – galaxies millions of times further apart than stars

Our galaxy (Milky Way) would look like this from space

Life of a star

- **Birth – dust + gas** —immense gravity—> star
- **Mass – very large** compared to planets
- **Volume** – Sun (small star) million times larger volume than Earth
- **Density** – star matter **millions of times denser than Earth** matter
- **Heat** – stars are balls of **very hot gases**
  – creates forces tending to **expansion** of Star
  – forces balance —> **stability** (e.g. our Sun)
- **Size change – stable** for millions of years
  – **expansion** —> **red giant** —> **rapid contraction** —> **supernova explosion**

red giant ↓ **contraction** ↓ **white dwarf** (very small, cold)

supernova explosion ↓ **neutron star** (very dense) ↓ **black hole** (no light escapes)

Make sure your answers only contain the key important points

Energy production in a star

- **Light nuclei – fuse** —> **heavier nuclei**
  – **vast energy release**
  – present in Sun/inner planets —> solar system formed from explosions of old stars

Nuclear fusion is not the same process as nuclear fission (which occurs in nuclear power stations)

^2_1H + ^2_1H → ^4_2He + ENERGY

heavy hydrogen (deuterium) — helium nucleus

Origin of Universe

- **Red shift – light** from other galaxies **shifted to red** end of spectrum
- **More red shift – galaxies further away** —> galaxies **receding fast** —> universe **expanding**
- **Big Bang – theory** on possible start of universe
- – **uses red shift observations**
- – **universe began from explosion of matter**
- **Age – at least 15 billion years old**

Some scientists believe that the Universe has always existed – this is called the Steady State theory

The Earth & beyond

Questions

1 One use of artificial satellites is to broadcast information around the world.

a) What is the name we give to this type of satellite? ______________________

b) Name and describe the use of one other type of satellite.

____

____

2 Astronauts in an orbiting spacecraft experience weightlessness.

a) What does this mean?

____

b) The spacecraft is still within the gravitational field of the Earth. Explain why the astronauts are weightless.

____

____

3 Halley's comet is seen in the sky every 75 years.

a) With the aid of a diagram explain why it is seen only periodically and not all the time.

b) On your diagram draw the path of a second comet that would only ever be seen once from the Earth.

4 Describe the stages in the evolution of a star resulting in the formation of a neutron star.

____

____

____

____

____

____

Energy Resources & Energy Transfer

Thermal energy

- **Thermal energy** – transferred from **hot to cold body**

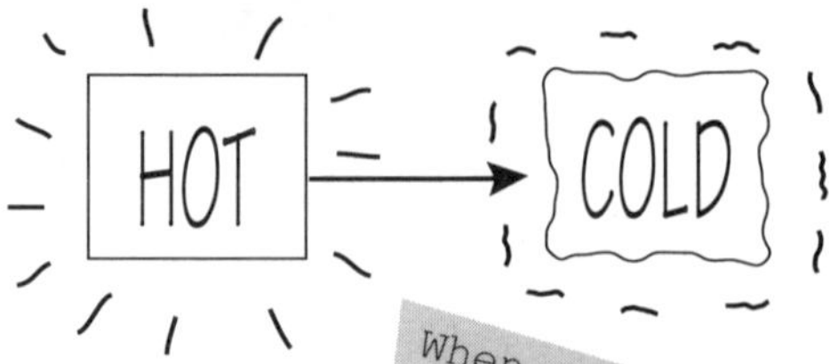

When you open an outside door, you're letting the heat out – not the cold in!

Conduction

- **Adjacent particles transfer energy**
- **Metal – good conductor**
  - **hotter —> more kinetic energy (KE)** for free electrons —> **diffusion**
  - **also energy transfer by collision**
- **Non-metals/liquids – poor conductors**
- **Gases – very poor conductors**

Convection

You should know about sources of heat loss from e.g. home, cup of tea + ways of reducing the loss by insulation

- **Gas/liquid – particles gain KE —> expansion**
  - **hotter parts** less dense —> **rise up**
  - **colder parts** more dense —> **replace hotter parts**
- **Examples – hot air balloon, sea breeze**

Most heat loss from a building is via the roof

Radiation

- **Energy transfer by waves**
- **Part of electromagnetic spectrum** (infra-red, IR)
- **Emission – hot bodies**
  - **dark, matt surfaces**

An open fire mainly heats a room by creating a convection current. You have to be very near to feel the radiated heat.

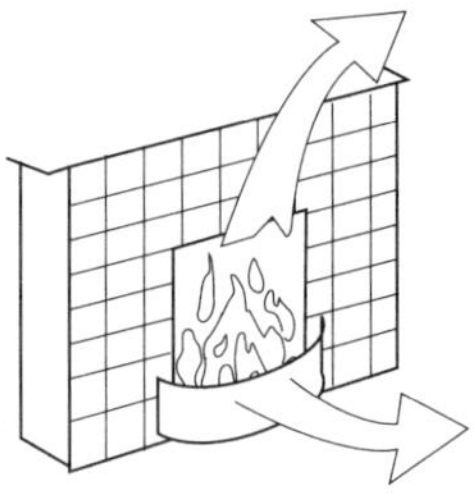

Energy efficiency

Efficiency	=	useful energy transferred / total energy supplied

$$\text{Efficiency} = \frac{\text{useful energy transferred}}{\text{total energy supplied}}$$

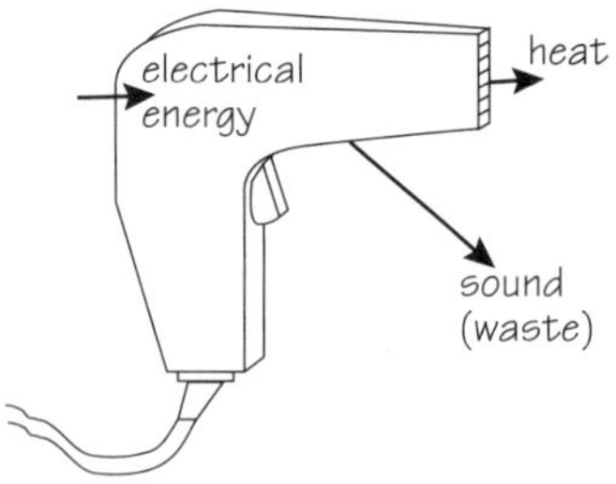

- **Unuseful energy – wasted**
  - **reduces efficiency**
- **Energy supplied – heats surroundings**
  - increasingly **spread out**
  - **more difficult to use for energy transfer**

Energy resources

- **Renewable** – will not run out, e.g. wood, tides, wind.
- **Non-renewable** – cannot be replaced, e.g. fossil fuels, nuclear.
- **Power station** – generates **electricity from both types.**
- **Steam** – produced by **non-renewable** resources + **wood/geothermal**
  - drives turbines.
- **Turbines – driven directly by renewable resources**
  - **solar cells** produce **electricity directly**
  - **turn generators —> electricity**

fuel → BOILER → steam → TURBINE → GENERATOR → ELECTRICITY

Chemical energy → Thermal energy → Kinetic energy → Electrical energy

Non-Renewable vs Renewable

Non-Renewable

- Will **run out**
- **Waste**
- **Fuel costs**
- **Transportation**
- **Building costs** high

Renewable

- Will **not run out**
- **No waste**
- **No fuel costs**
- **No transportation**
- **Generating equipment costs** high (note: above excludes wood)

Work

Work done = force × distance
= energy transferred

- **Units – joules (J)**
- **1 J – 1 Nm**

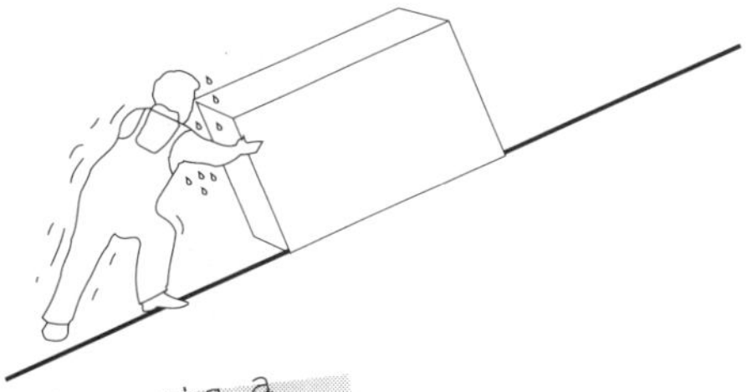

A ramp is a machine. Machines make work easier. Other examples include: spanner, pulley, lever

Power = work done/time taken
= rate of energy transfer

- **Units – watts (W)**
- **1 W – 1 J/s**

Kinetic energy (KE)

Students often forget that speed must be squared

- **Moving** object has KE
- **KE depends on mass and speed**

KE = 1/2 × mass × (speed)²

- **Units – J**
- **Example – moving car**

A high diver exchanges her PE for KE on the way down

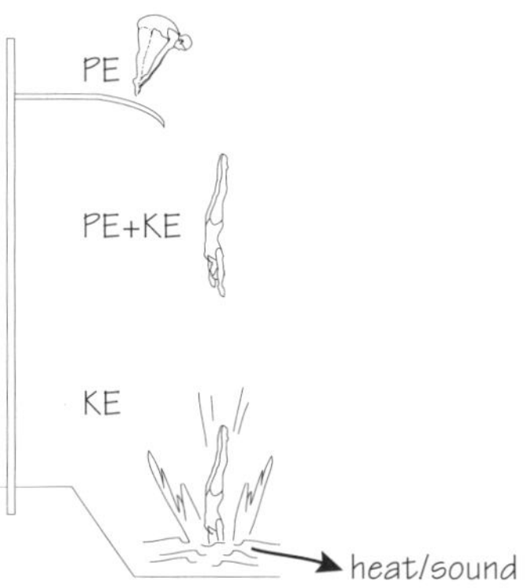

Potential energy (PE)

- **Gravitational PE – energy stored**
  - **– depends on weight + height**
  - **– example: walking upstairs**

Gravitational PE =
weight × change in vertical height

- **Units – J**
- **Weight depends on**
  - **– mass**
  - **– gravitational field strength, *g***

Weight = mass X *g*

- **Gravitational field strength** – on **Earth** about **10 N/kg**
  – on **Moon** about **1.7 N/kg**
- **Elastic PE – energy stored**
  - **– depends on** change in **shape** of body
  - **– examples: stretched spring, catapult**

Energy resources & energy transfer

Questions

1 A 'radiator' used in home central heating should really be called a 'convector'. Do you agree? Explain your answer.

____

____

2 An electric kettle is rated at 1 kW.
It takes 30 s to heat up a certain mass of water.

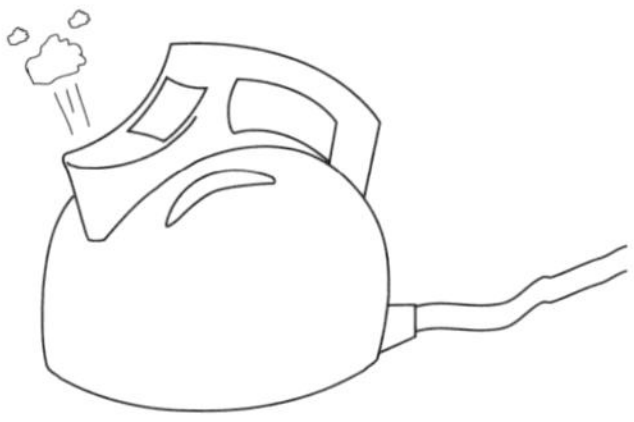

a) If 1 W = 1 J/s, how much energy is supplied to the kettle?

____

b) 10 kJ of energy is wasted. Calculate the efficiency of the kettle.

____

c) i) How is this energy wasted? ______________________________

ii) How could this waste be reduced? ______________________________

3 a) Name a renewable energy resource. ______________________________

b) Describe three main advantages that renewable energy resources have over non-renewable resources for the generation of electricity.

i) ______________________________

ii) ______________________________

iii) ______________________________

4 Julie runs up a staircase. Each step is 20 cm high. There are 10 steps to the top. If her weight is 450 N,

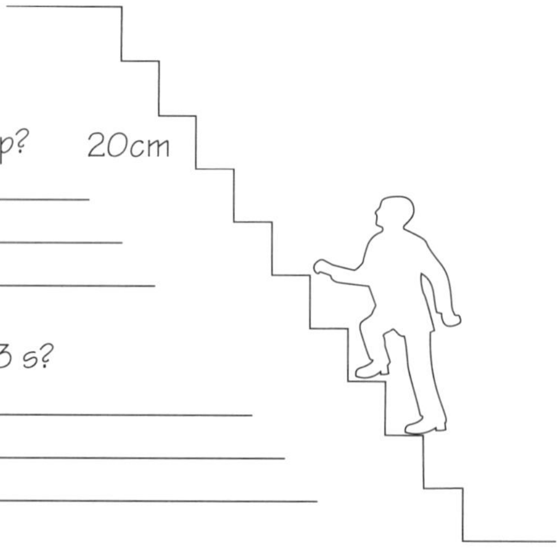

a) how much work must she do to reach the top?

____

____

____

b) what power does she develop if it takes her 3 s?

____

____

____

Radioactivity

Atomic structure

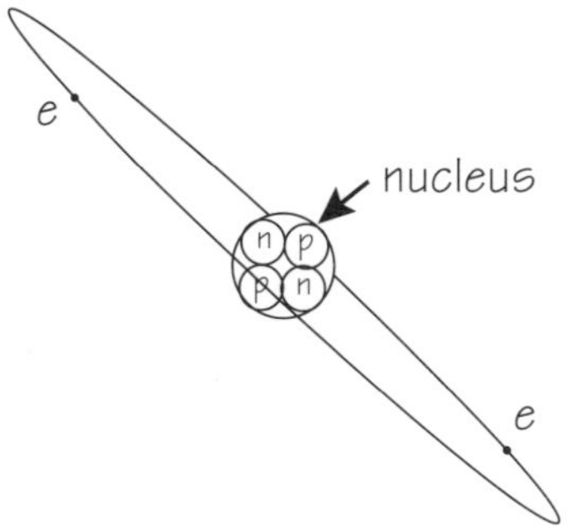

- **Atoms** – **tiny** central **nucleus**
- **Radioactivity** – *emitted* when **nucleus changes**
- **Nucleus** – **protons** (**p**) + **neutrons** (**n**)
- **Electrons** (**e**) – **orbit around nucleus**
- **Plum pudding model** – **plums** (**electrons**) **embedded** in atom
- **Alpha scattering** —> **nucleus** has positive (**+**) **charge**

	Mass	Charge
p	1	+1
n	1	0
e	negligible	–1

Number of p = number of e overall charge on atom is zero

Elements

Nucleon number minus proton number gives number of neutrons

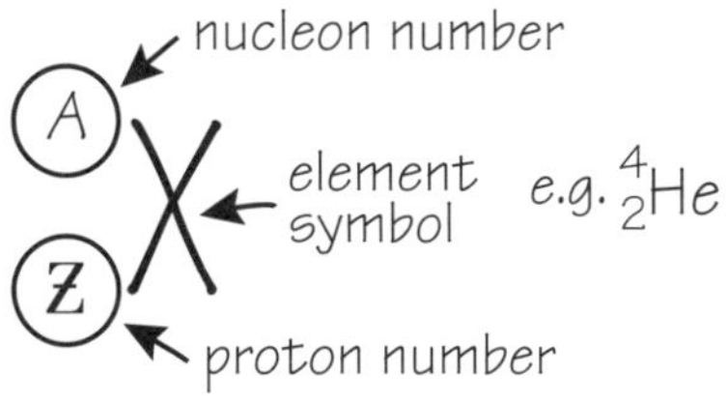

- **Proton number** – **same** for atoms of **same element**
- **Nucleon** (**mass**) **number** – total **number of p + n**
- **Isotope** – atoms of **same element** with **different** number of **n**
- **Radioactive isotope** – isotopes with **unstable nuclei**
  – also known as **radioisotope** or **radionuclide**
- **Disintegration** – **nucki break up** —> number of **n may change** —> **different element**
- **Radiation emission** – **continually**
  – **random**

Types of radiation

Note that γ decay has no affect on nucleon or proton number

Look at composition to predict new proton and nucleon numbers

Type	Symbol	Stopped by	Composition	Charge	Mass
alpha	α	thin sheet of paper	2p+2n (He nucleus)	+	large
beta	ß	2 cm air/2 mm metal	electrons; n—> p + e	–	tiny
gamma	γ	reduced by thick concrete/lead	Em radiation	0	0

Sources of radiation

Radiation is a natural part of our environment; it is called 'background radiation'

- **Space** – *cosmic rays*
- **Ground/building materials**
- **Food**
- **Medical** – radiography, e.g. chest X-ray
  – treatment e.g. cancer
- **Nuclear power station**

Dangers of radiation

- **Absorption** by material —> **ionisation** of atoms
- **Cell damage** – **may kill/cause cancer**
  – alpha most dangerous in body
  – beta, gamma most dangerous outside body

Uses of radiation

- **Monitor/control thickness** – greater absorption by thicker material
  – alpha and beta
- **Medical treatment** – kill cancer cells
  – gamma
- **Tracers** – trace path of fluids

GM tube measures activity

Half-life

In practise, background count should be subtracted

- **Radioactive atoms** —> **radiation** —> **stable** (non-radioactive atoms)
- **Activity decreases with time**
- **Half-life** – **time** for activity/count rate **to halve**
  – different for different radioisotopes e.g. Na–24 is 15 hours, Pt–239 is 24000 years
- **Carbon dating** – half-life 5730 years
  – used to find **age of radioactive material**

The graph shows the decay of a radionuclide. Half-life = t

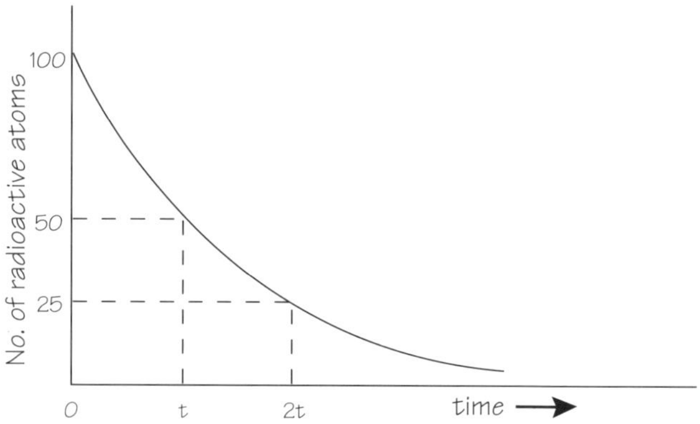

Nuclear fission

- **Neutrons** – **fired at large nucleus**
- **Nucleus splits** —> neutrons released
  —> **chain**

reaction

- **New atoms also radioactive**
- **Energy released** – **much larger than** associated with a **chemical bond**
- **Nuclear power stations release energy by nuclear fission**
- **Sun releases energy by nucl**

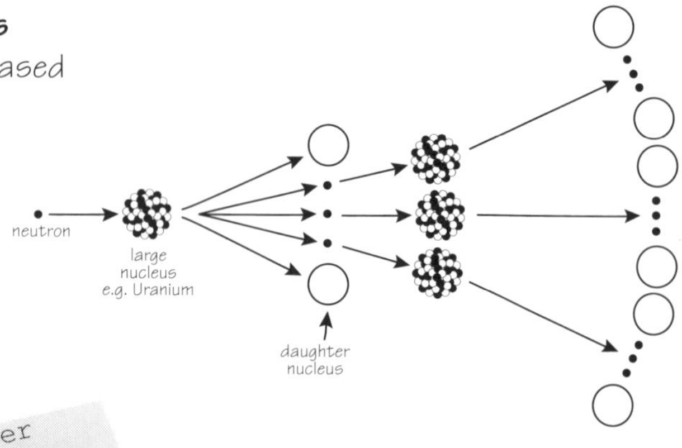

In a nuclear power station, the chain reaction is slowed/stopped by control rods; they absorb the neutrons.

Radioactivity Questions

1 a) Explain the 'plum pudding' model of the atom.

b) How was this model modified from the alpha scattering experiments?

2 Name two ways in which gamma radiation differs from either alpha or beta radiation.

i)

ii)

3 The activity of a sample of a radionuclide was measured. It was found to be 3000 counts/min at 9 am. By 11 am this had decreased to 750 counts/min.

a) What instrument is used to measure the activity?

b) Calculate the half-life of the sample.

c) When the detector was moved away, the experimenter noticed that it still recorded a low count rate. Why?

4 Steel sheets are produced in a steel mill. The sheets are rolled out to a certain thickness as they pass along a conveyor belt. By drawing a diagram, explain how a radioactive source can be used to monitor and control the thickness.

Physical processes • Answers

Electricity & magnetism

1 Negative charges on rod – transfer to cloth – makes cloth –ve and rod +ve

2 a) 6 V b) Current through each lamp = 1.5 A

$R = V/I$

$= 6/1.5$

$= 4\Omega$

c) R increases as filament heats up – measure R when lamp on for e.g. 30 s, when filament reaches highest temperature

3 a) $I = P/V$

$= 1500/250$

$= 6$ A

Use 10 A fuse

b) 7 days @ ⅓ hour per day = 7/3 hours

Cost = $1.5 \times 7/3 \times 6$p

= 21 p

4 a) Output voltage bigger than input voltage

b) Number of turns needed =

$\frac{7.0}{2.0} \times 100 = 350$

5 a) Divides up the battery voltage; pd shared between components

b) Thermistor heated

—> resistance decreases

—> pd across thermistor decreases ($V \propto R$)

—> pd across transistor decreases

—> transistor switches off

—> LED goes out

Forces & motion

1 a) Constant acceleration

b) i) Acceleration = 6/30

$= 0.2$ m/s^2

ii) distance = area under graph

= area of triangle

$= \frac{1}{2} \times 30 \times 6$

= 90 m

2 a) Resultant force = 6500 – 850

= 5650 N

Acceleration = F/m

= 5650/1200

= 4.71 m/s^2

b) Reaction time, weather, condition of tyres/brakes/road

3 ⅕ of beam's length = 0.5 m

↷ moment = 120×0.5

= 60 Nm

↶ moment = $W \times 1.25$

= $1.25W$ Nm

To balance, $1.25W = 60$

$W = 48$ N

4 Momentum before collision

$= 5000 \times 10 + 3000 \times 5$

= 50 000 + 15 000

= 65 000 kgm/s

Momentum after collision

$= 8000 \times v$ kgm/s

Conservation of momentum —>

$8000\,v = 65\,000$

$v = 8.13$ m/s

5 Force $= \frac{0.4}{0.1} \times 150$

$= 4 \times 150$

= 600 N

Waves

1 a) i) Wavelength = 2.45 cm
ii) Amplitude = 0.65 cm

b) i) 1½ wavelengths fit on screen in 0.01 s
so, 1 wavelength takes 2/3 × 0.01 s

$$\text{frequency} = \frac{1}{\frac{2}{3} \times 0.01} = 3/0.02 = 150\ \text{Hz}$$

ii) Speed = 150 x 2.7
= 405 m/s

2 a)

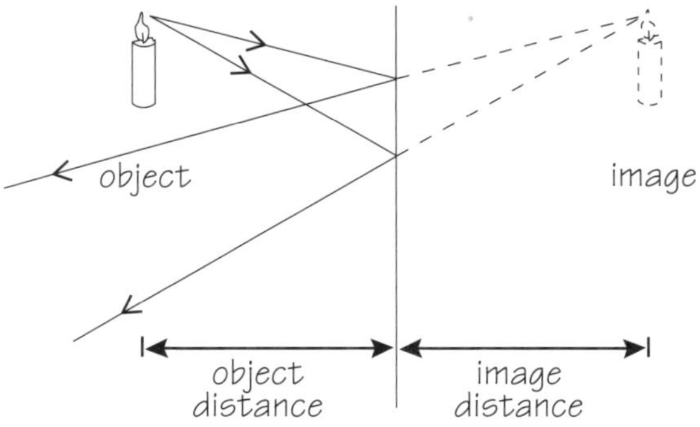

b) Virtual. Not really there/cannot be projected on a screen.

3 a) (Ultrasonic) pulse sent into water
Time to return to receiver measured
Depth of shoal = speed × time

b) 0.3 s for signal to travel there and back
Use time = 0.15 s
Depth = 1550 × 0.15
= 232.5 m

4 P – longitudinal – fast – travel through solids + liquids
S – transverse – slow – travel only through solids

The Earth & beyond

1 a) Communications satellite
b) Monitoring – gather Earth data on e.g. weather observatory – gather space data on e.g. planets

2 a) No weight.
b) Spacecraft pulled towards Earth by gravitational force
Astronauts pulled towards spacecraft
Floor falls away as fast as astronauts fall toward floor
No contact with floor
Therefore zero weight

3 a) Long elliptical orbit
only visible when near Earth

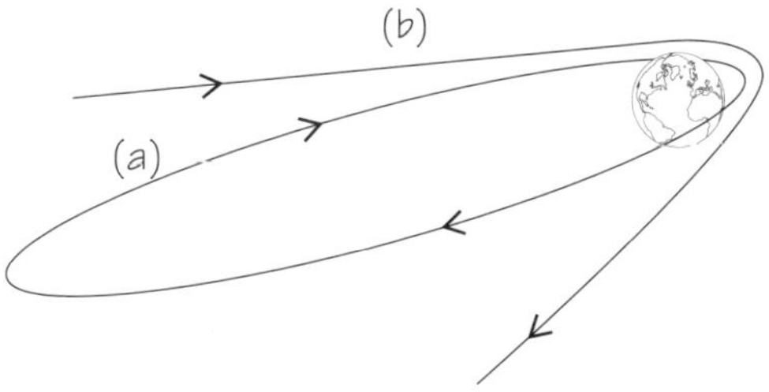

b) Parabolic path – never returns.
(NB not comet burns up in atmosphere!)

4 Dust + gas —> star born
↓
stability —> expansion
↓
red giant —> rapid contraction —> supernova
↓
neutron star

Energy resources & energy transfer

1 Yes – little radiated heat – room mainly heated by creation of convection current

2 a) 1kW = 1000 W
Energy supplied = 1000 × 30 s
= 30000 J
= 30 kJ

b) Efficiency = $\frac{10\ kJ}{30\ kJ} \times 100$
= 33 %

c) i) Heats up kettle body/surroundings sound energy produced
ii) Insulate kettle e.g. wrap insulation around

3 a) Any of wind, wave, tidal, geothermal, solar, wood
b) Will not run out, no waste, no fuel cost, no transportation cost

4 a) Work = force × distance
= 450 × 10 × 0.2
= 900 J

b) Power = $\frac{\text{work done}}{\text{time taken}}$

= 900/3
= 300 W

Radioactivity

1 a) Plums = electrons
electrons embedded in atom
b) Atom has central nucleus
nucleus tiny
nucleus + ve
electrons orbit nucleus
most of atom empty space

2 Gamma – wave not particle
– no mass/charge
– travels at speed of light/ 3×10^8 m/s

3 a) GM tube/counter
b) 9am – 3000 counts/min
11am – 750 counts/min
Therefore 2 hours —> drops to ¼
1 hour —> drops to ½
half-life = 1 hour
c) Recording background radiation

4 radioactive source

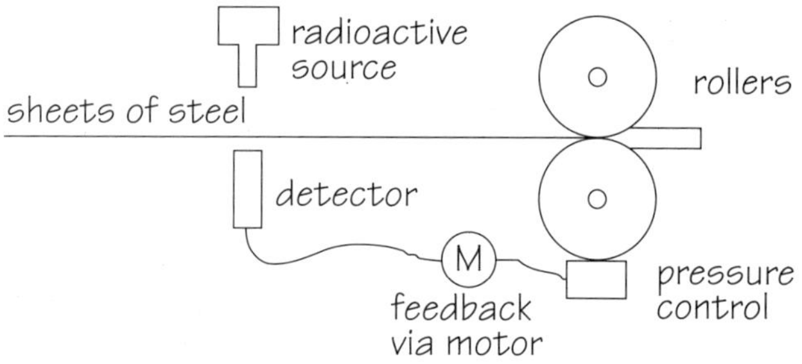

Source above/below sheets
detector below/above sheets
correct thickness ——> p counts/min recorded
thickness too big ——> less than p recorded
thickness too small ——> more than p recorded
link detector via feedback to motor
motor controls roller pressure